MW00777409

LIQUIDITY AND YOU:™

A Personal Guide for Tech and Business Entrepreneurs Approaching an Exit

Nicole,

Congrats on the success.

LIQUIDITY AND YOU:™

A PERSONAL GUIDE FOR TECH AND BUSINESS ENTREPRENEURS APPROACHING AN EXIT

ANTHONY GLOMSKI

Liquidity & You
A Personal Guide for Tech and Business Entrepreneurs Approaching an Exit

By Anthony Glomski

Skyridge Press books may be purchased for special sales, business or promotional use. For further information, please contact the publisher at www.skyridgepress.com.

Printed in the United States of America.

Jacket Design by Monika Daužickaitė.

Cataloging and Publication Data is on file with the publisher.

ISBN-13: 978-0-9991041-9-4

Distributed to the trade by Thomson-Shore.

skyridgepress.com

To my dad—who taught me that
while analysis can help me understand life,
compassion creates the meaning of life.

WHAT READERS SAY: LIQUIDITY AND YOU

"Change is constant, challenges are inevitable, and the only way to survive is to create a solid support team around you and never give up. As you exit a business, change careers, or prepare for the next chapter in your life, curiosity and your attitude will be paramount to this transition or any other in your life. . . . This book is a perfect place to start that journey."

—Brian Vickers, NASCAR Driver

"In *Liquidity & You*, Anthony has created a comprehensive guide based on significant real-world experiences. Whether the sale of your business is two years or 20 years in the future, it's important to be aware in advance of the areas on which you need to focus. Anthony sheds light on strategies that will help you prepare for the future instead of being forced to react to events that have already taken place. Decades of experience serving clients with highly complex situations has taught me the importance of the Personal CFO. The proper group of trusted advisors working for you in a coordinated manner can be invaluable. What Anthony presents in *Liquidity & You* is not theory; it has actually been tested and shown to work."

—Jim Carlin, Founder & Partner, Holthouse Carlin & Van Trigt LLP

"Anthony Glomski's *Liquidity & You* is a must read for any entrepreneur who has had or will have a liquidity event. Glomski's book vividly illustrates why planning is so critical for this demographic. I've worked with many entrepreneurs who are brilliant at creating wealth, but I have also seen what a huge difference methodical planning can make. There are many things entrepreneurs can do to preserve and enhance their wealth even prior to liquidity events, which Glomski discusses in great detail."

—Chirag Chotalia, Venture Capitalist, Draper Fisher Jurvetson; Former VC Pritzker Family Office

"On my way to winning five Olympic medals, I abided by a fundamental rule: Find a coach you can trust and follow the coach's instructions without hesitation. In business vernacular, it's 'follow the process.' In his book *Liquidity & You*, Anthony Glomski's outline of what a financial coach should prescribe is a most revealing and helpful plan for maintaining and maximizing your family's wealth. I especially appreciated his use of helpful metaphors, entertaining quotes, and pertinent statistics to make the complicated material consistently interesting. I was a great swimmer, but it did not necessarily mean that I was good at creating the best workouts for me. In fact, I am rather relieved that I did not bear that responsibility as well. Just because you were good at creating wealth does not mean that you are the best person to manage that wealth. For that, a team of the right expert advisors will both take away the doubt and free up lots of time to do other things. If you're looking for gold-medal results, read *Liquidity & You* and follow Anthony's advice."

—John Naber, Olympic Champion, Author, Speaker, and Network Sports Announcer

"A liquidity event creates opportunities, but in my experience it also amplified financial decisions, created new priorities, and exposed potential pitfalls. Listening to others who have built companies and looking for professionals who fit well is a process. Anthony's experience helps by providing insight and a foundation, removing pre- and post-exit blind spots. *Liquidity & You* identifies the right questions to ask yourself, other entrepreneurs, and future advisors."

—Paul Glomski, Co-Founder and CEO, Detroit Labs

"The punchline of Anthony's book is that a lot of very smart and talented professionals create wealth but do not seek professional advice on how to protect their wealth. Good estate planners, money managers, lawyers, personal CFOs, and in some cases even good therapists can make up a great team to create the best long-term results."

—Brian Stevens, CEO, ConferenceDirect

"Anthony Glomski's *Liquidity & You* is a succinct meditation on why, in the world of wealth management, preservation of wealth is paramount. 'Preserve your wealth' will be your mantra after reading this informative book that gives you the formula on how this can be achieved."

—Jason Trenton, Tax and Wealth Planning Partner, Venable LLP

TABLE OF CONTENTS

FOREWORD

I want to start by thanking Anthony for inviting me to contribute in a small way to this book. The topics that follow are very close to my heart for many reasons. Let's just say that challenges and transitions are something that I'm very familiar with.

I started my life in Thomasville, North Carolina, born to two amazing parents, Ramona and Clyde, along with my sister, Melissa. I had a great upbringing, with a huge focus on family, fun, sports, the outdoors and education. I didn't have a lot of restrictions or rules as I aged, but the ones I had were enforced strictly. Bringing home solid grades was at the top of the list. I believe this combination instilled a deep sense of independence, curiosity, creativity and knowledge in me.

Don't get me wrong—I was a complete handful, or so I was told! My grandmother's nickname for me was "Incorrigible." In case you were curious about the definition of that word, it means "impervious to correction through discipline."

As I have traveled through life, I have come to realize a couple of important lessons. Top among them is balance. Life requires balance, and it will demand it of you if you're not willing to find it on your own. This includes balancing your strengths and weaknesses, which I have personally often found tend to be one and the same. Curiosity without question is probably my greatest strength and my greatest weakness. All my strengths contributed to my successes and to my nickname, because they are also my weaknesses.

Ken Howes, a very wise man, once told me when I was racing at Hendrick Motorsports: "There are three things you can count on in life: you will be born, you will die and everything will change in between."

He told me this shortly after I found myself dealing with one of the biggest challenges in my life. My best friend, Ricky Hendrick, passed away on my 21st birthday. He was not only my friend but also the owner of my racecar, and we had just won the NASCAR Busch Series Championship in our first year together. Ken's quote has stuck with me since then.

There is one other quote that has helped me a lot as I move through life—one that my father told me time and again: "Never Give Up." I don't think he ever knew how important it would be. Or maybe he did?

My highs have been amazing! They include racing professionally across the world at over 200 mph and winning races and championships at the highest level of sports, having the support of an amazing wife, family, friends and colleagues along the way. But my lows have been, well, let's say amazing too! I have had blood clots four times, heart surgery twice and open-heart surgery once. I could have died during any of those experiences, and really should have died during two of them. There's nothing like having one hour to say good-bye to your loved ones before an emergency open-heart surgery to put things in perspective. Not to mention dealing with all that while changing careers, at first slowly, and then abruptly— going from motorsports to the worlds of TV and finance.

It was all amazing, though! I learned so much through these ups and downs. They all contributed to who I am today and my successes. As I like to say now, "What doesn't kill you makes you stronger, but everything in the middle sucks!"

I have been very blessed to pull off this transition suc-cessfully due to the team that I assembled or, I should say, assembled around me. First and foremost, the most important partner in my life: my kind, wise, understand-ing, patient and amazing wife, Sarah! My outstanding and unwavering parents and family! The best, wisest and most honest mentor I could ever ask for, David Sokol. A brilliant sports psychologist, Jack Stark. Two great financial advisors, Peter Savarino and Adam Landau. My two brilliant business partners at Crown Predator Holdings, Nick Lewin and Justin Kamm. Not to mention all the great friends along the way that gave me incredible advice and friendship, starting with Tommy Kendall. He's one of my closest friends but also

> What doesn't kill you makes you stronger, but everything in the middle sucks!

my personal life coach, even though he probably doesn't know this and certainly didn't sign up for that role!

I bring all this up because I think it relates to this book in some very meaningful ways. Change is constant, challenges are inevitable, and the only way to survive is to create a solid support team around you and Never Give Up! As you exit a business, change careers or prepare for the next chapter in your life, curiosity and your attitude will be paramount to this transition or any other in your life. Be prepared to go to school again with an empty bucket, just like you had when you were young. It's unlikely that much of what made you successful in your prior career will carry over. Certainly the wisdom you gained as a person will, but the knowledge and experience that made you the best in that business will have to be relearned. Be prepared to make mistakes, but never give up. No one will care more about your wealth and your family's long-term well-being than you do!

This book is a perfect place to start that journey. I have a lot of respect for Anthony personally and professionally. I thoroughly enjoyed and learned a lot from reading this book. I'm confident you will as well.

Now empty your bucket and start reading…

Brian Vickers
NASCAR Driver

WHY READ THIS BOOK?

If you take away nothing else from this book, I want you to understand that you can make an impact with your money. You can significantly change your life, your children's lives and the lives of the people who benefit from your charitable pursuits. No matter what, you're the CFO of your own family. After reading this book, you can continue being your own CFO, or you can begin to work with someone else. As a successful entrepreneur, you have the kind of vision and passion that drive you to make a dent in the universe. By aligning that passion with the process we'll be laying out in this book, you'll increase your odds of making that impact. Think of this book as a starting place for building, preserving and responsibly sharing your wealth.

Since you are an entrepreneur, your financial life is more complicated than the average person's. You likely have many "moving parts" to manage and coordinate. You own a company. You have an equity stake, stock options or other early-stage deferred compensation. You may have trademarks, commercial buildings, parcels of land, art collections and nonqualified deferred compensation plans, along with more traditional assets such as stocks and bonds. You may have a large extended family that you care about deeply and for which you want the best. And you may want to devote some of your resources to your favorite cause (or even start your own foundation to maximize your philanthropy).

> Think of this book as a starting place for building, preserving and responsibly sharing your wealth.

These complexities require a solution for managing your wealth that helps provide much-needed clarity—a process that coordinates all of these moving parts to ensure that they are working in concert with each other. This way you can create the ideal financial outcomes for you and your family.

In the pages that follow, we'll address key investment concerns such as building the optimal portfolio to grow your unique assets. We'll also go beyond your investment portfolio to explore the best ways to **protect, enhance, transfer** and **donate your money**. These efforts need to be carefully coordinated so that the decisions made in one area complement (and don't hinder) the efforts made in any others. This is where we feel our firm makes the biggest impact for our clients.

By using the **Collaborative Wealth Management Process** detailed in this book, you should be able to achieve not only great financial success, but peace of mind for yourself and your family. As an advisor, I use the Collaborative Wealth Management Process every day to help my clients realize their personal, professional and financial goals.

I care very deeply about helping entrepreneurs and their

families with their wealth so they can secure the peace of mind they need to do the things that they love—such as being with their families, working on their businesses, helping charities and exiting on their own terms. Our Collaborative Wealth Management Process is the best approach I know to help make that happen.

What are some of the unique financial and social needs of entrepreneurs today? I invite you to flip to the next chapter to find out. Later you'll also learn how the Collaborative Wealth Management Process will enable you to create and enjoy a life of fulfillment, comfort and security.

MY PERSONAL STORY

You should be proud of your achievements. Whether you own a medical practice or you helped develop an app for a company approaching an IPO, starting and growing your business has never been easy. You have overcome obstacles, transcended personal doubt and created possibilities for yourself and your company when others told you repeatedly it couldn't be done. You're a motivator and a creator.

Despite your accomplishments, you know you've still got more to achieve. You need to ensure that you do whatever it takes to preserve, protect and maintain the wealth that you have worked so hard to build. Going forward, you'll be met with new challenges, new transitions and new opportunities—many of which may feel unpredictable. The decisions you make during these key moments will have a huge impact on your quality of life and the lives of those you care about. Your goal? Maximize what you've created so that you can make your dent in the universe.

Making smart choices about your money is vital to accomplishing what you want in life, now and in the future. To make that happen, you need a comprehensive strategy. You need to manage all aspects of your wealth with a strategy that takes into account each piece of your financial life. You need a coordinated plan ensuring that your financial life is aligned with your core values and most meaningful goals.

That is what this book is all about. It is designed to give you—a successful business owner or tech entrepreneur approaching a liquidity event—the tools you need to thrive in the next chapter of your life. These tools will help you identify your goals and position your wealth to turn your vision into reality—for yourself, for your family, for your community and for the causes you deeply care about.

MY PATH TO HELPING ENTREPRENEURS

As many of you know, I am an entrepreneur and have several close relatives who are successful entrepreneurs. Like some of you, I had a modest upbringing and had tremendous fear about money as a kid. My dad never had much job security. He was an engineer at a naval base that was constantly under the threat of closure—a common occurrence in the 1980s and 1990s—and my mom had ongoing heart issues that prevented her from working.

The early messaging I got from my mother was: "We are in trouble; there is not enough money. You may not be able to go back to school. Your father could lose his job and we can't afford to buy a new car." As it turned out, my parents weren't paranoid. The naval base where my dad worked was ultimately closed. Luckily a publicly traded company (GM Hughes) came along and acquired the base. My dad kept his job, but he lost more than half of his pension. As a result, the fear of scarcity always loomed large in our house. I responded in two ways: (1) I went out and made money, and (2) I learned as much as I possibly could about preserving the money I made. I never ever wanted to feel that sense of scarcity again.

Life can throw a lot of struggle and hardship our way. While a healthy financial picture won't solve all your concerns, it can certainly help you navigate those difficult moments.

My own journey to helping self-made people make smart choices about their money began during my childhood in Indianapolis. At age 11, I started mowing lawns and cleaning gutters. I also bought candy in bulk and then sold individual pieces at my school for a profit. I did whatever I could do to make a buck. Simultaneously, I wanted to learn everything I could about personal finance, a topic that is rarely addressed within our school systems. I wanted to make that feeling of scarcity go away, not just for me, but among my peers. We all deserve access to the tools required for creating security for ourselves.

A buddy of mine who has an MBA from an Ivy League school was embarrassed to ask for help with his portfolio. Don't feel bad about not knowing what you weren't taught. Our school systems have failed us.

Fortunately, I had some good role models. My

grandfather owned two full-service gas stations. I remember that he always greeted customers by name, filled their tank and cleaned their windows without thinking twice about it. He owned and operated a "service station" with an emphasis on the word "service." Those establishments provided a nice life for my mom's family and made them respected within the community.

In terms of self-education, I've always been curious about how things work. My father's engineering background must have rubbed off on me, as some of my earliest childhood memories are of taking apart old black-and-white televisions (color was too expensive) and attaching speakers from a Sony boom box to make "stereo TV." I always wanted to see what was on the inside of things, and how all the mechanical innards fit together.

This inquisitiveness was especially helpful when relying on 10-year-old cars—batteries, alternators, starters, etc. I wasn't a great student growing up, but I was smart in a practical way. My high school guidance counselor, Mrs. Hannigan, didn't think I was college material. She called me into her office one day and urged me to think about becoming an electrician or a plumber because she knew I enjoyed working with my hands. Once again, I felt that fear of scarcity. What I heard her telling me was "you will always be poor," and I felt a lot of guilt because my parents had taken a loan to send me to a college prep school.

What Mrs. Hannigan didn't know was that I had been working up to 30 hours every week at a Subway sandwich shop since the age of 14. Instead of spending time studying, I was learning firsthand what it was like to run a business (in this case a franchise, since the owner had three Subway shops). Still, that meeting with Mrs. Hannigan was a big turning point for me. The fear of that scarcity motivated me to buckle down and focus on school so I could get into college.

I worked hard, and it paid off. I was accepted to Xavier University in Cincinnati. I started out in pre-med because my dad wanted me to be a doctor or a teacher—i.e., someone who could help people. He didn't want me to be a "greedy capitalist." But I took some business classes and discovered that they seemed much easier for me than pre-med. I felt like accounting was the science behind business, and I'd always be able to get a job. Since Xavier is a private Jesuit university, all students (including the business majors) were required to take philosophy, ethics and other mind-opening courses to help us understand the importance of service in the world. That made my dad happy and helped him live with my decision not to become a doctor or a teacher. However, my mom's philosophy was that you should always follow the entrepreneurial path. So I had some work to do if I was going to keep both of my parents happy—and myself.

FROM ACCOUNTING FIRM TO TRADING PIT

In the end, I graduated from Xavier with honors and got a job as an accountant in the Chicago office of one of biggest accounting firms in the world. At age 22, I was working with both public and privately held companies, and had the opportunity to interface with CFOs and CEOs right out of the gate. *Not bad for a kid whose guidance counselor didn't think he should go to college.* As you'll see later in this book, the CFO's role as the "financial quarterback" of an organization is something that has stayed with me to this day.

I was young and healthy. I had a great job and a great career in a great city. Yet I still felt a void in my life. The only part of my job that I really liked was looking into the investment side of the balance sheets of the companies I was auditing. I enjoyed working with the CFOs of our client companies, but as I looked at my elder peers at my accounting firm, I realized the life of a Big Four partner was not for me. I sensed there could be something more to my life than long hours doing audits six or seven days a week.

A friend of mine likes to say, "If you hang out in a barber shop long enough, sooner or later you will end up getting a haircut." Eventually, I ended up on an assignment for my accounting firm that was directly across from the Chicago Board of Trade (CBOT). During my lunch hour (or half hour), I'd go to the CBOT's observation deck and watch the traders in action. It was mesmerizing. I decided that no matter what, I was going to find a way to work down in "the pit" and be at the epicenter of the financial markets.

Eventually I landed a job on the trading floor at the Chicago Board of Options Exchange (CBOE). I was surrounded by an amazing group of highly intelligent misfits who spent their days yelling and screaming at each other. What's interesting about the culture of the pit is that it tends to be populated by very smart people who have a math orientation—physicists, mathematicians, doctors, lawyers—but who just didn't want to work (or who can't work) in the mainstream corporate world. The pit was controlled, calculated chaos—and I loved it.

I was recruited to the CBOE by a couple of brilliant guys, one of whom was a CPA and Harvard MBA. I quickly discovered that successful options traders made significantly more money than partners at accounting firms. Success was contingent primarily on controlling risk and costs. If they meditated (and many did), their mantra would be "preserve your wealth." Discipline, drive and a relentless focus on preserving wealth afforded these guys a great lifestyle. While some believe options trading is essentially gambling, it's actually very far from gambling. In reality, the successful traders were the "house," while everyone else was gambling. The traders I knew had children and families—they couldn't risk their livelihood by placing reckless bets. The lessons I learned in the pit would stick with me throughout my career.

MY INTRODUCTION TO TECH

In the late 1990s, the fear in the trading industry was that the human trading floor would be replaced by computers. So the firm's ultimate hedge was to go to Europe and open an office on a continent where trading had always been electronic. The idea was to develop software that would be the quickest on the market. It had to be fast because in trading, the first one in wins.

In reality, the successful traders were the "house," while everyone else was gambling. The traders I knew had children and families—they couldn't risk their livelihood by placing reckless bets.

The firm assigned me to its overseas operations to work with its accountants and lawyers in Switzerland, London and Frankfurt. Our head trader was a chemical engineer from Princeton with a Harvard MBA. We brought in Romanian programmers to develop high-speed software—measured down to the nanosecond—that was specifically designed for European options markets specializing in electronic trading. This was my formal introduction to the world of tech and a self-funded startup. At the time of the Daimler-Chrysler merger, there was a trade deal that flipped on a machine and made $1 million in one day. *Amazing*, I thought to myself. But, even then, I knew that the world of trading was on its way to being "disrupted." I had to pivot before getting crushed by the wave of change.

I always wanted to live in California, and I jumped at the first opportunity. I went to work for a proprietary trading firm there that traded exclusively **off** the floor. It was there that I met Brian Thomas, who, little did I know, would one day become my business partner and confidant—the way Charlie Munger is Warren Buffett's. Brian and I continue to work together closely to this day.

MY TRUE CALLING

Through most of the 2000s, I enjoyed living and working around the West Coast technology scene. But in 2001, when my mother passed away, my life changed. It became even more important for me to give back to society and to work on things that were meaningful. For example, I started counseling and advising people about their money issues. At first I did it just for fun, and for free. I loved helping people. And as bad as the tech crash of 2000 was, the 2008-2009 recession was even worse. It caused true financial devastation for many people, but it triggered something inside me. All the fears of scarcity I had as a kid came boiling to the surface. I saw people's lives change before my eyes.

I knew then that I *had* to help people. This was my call to action, and what I believe to be my calling in life. This was the catalyst that drove us to found our firm.

During the financial crisis, it was painful to see my friends' parents lose so much money. What made it especially sad was that they (and their "financial advisors") weren't following some very basic investment principles that could have significantly lessened their losses. Often, their advisors didn't really take the time to get to know them or any other clients, and so they didn't understand what their clients really wanted out of life.

In some cases, people were overconcentrated in single-name stocks like Lehman Brothers or Bear Stearns—companies that went away. This was a huge realized loss.

I wanted to prevent those outcomes, even though I've been surrounded by individuals at both tech companies and privately owned businesses whose wealth eggs were often highly concentrated in a single basket. While that seems to violate the laws of diversification, Andrew Carnegie actually encouraged people to keep all their eggs in one basket—and to watch the basket very carefully.

Having worked with individuals at both tech companies and privately owned businesses who have followed Carnegie's advice—and having seen the tremendous success that can come of it—I know that sometimes in life, you have to take calculated risks. But when it comes to your financial health, you want to preserve as much of your hard-earned wealth as you possibly can.

I have always been very conservative when it comes to taking risks. Perhaps it stems from my early career as an accountant or from my childhood immersed in a sense of scarcity, but at age 25 I got some highly valuable advice about wealth preservation. I was working as a convertible arbitrage trader in San Francisco, and my mentor told me: *"Get a nest egg, preserve your wealth, live cheaply and **stay in the game**."*

I was surrounded by people making tons of money in their 20s who were buying houses, cars and other big-ticket items. Then, suddenly, there would be a change in the market—namely, a thing called "algorithms"—and suddenly they would lose their ability to make money. Having spent much of their cash, they didn't have enough dry powder to stay in the game. My mentor's advice was so simplistic, yet so powerful. I saved and saved whatever money I earned, which in turn allowed me to grow.

> Get a nest egg, preserve your wealth, live cheaply and stay in the game.

In the pages that follow, I'll share many other valuable life lessons I learned from working closely with successful entrepreneurs and their families. I hope those lessons will prepare you for both the responsibilities and the great opportunities that your impending wealth will bring.

> I saved and saved whatever money I earned, which in turn allowed me to grow.

INTRODUCTION: MECHANIC VERSUS SALESMAN

Suppose you have a problem with your car and take it to your auto dealer. If you ask a salesperson what's wrong with your car, there is a high probability that he or she will try to sell you a new car. However, if you ask a mechanic what's wrong with your car, he or she will try to diagnose and fix it. I feel like I've spent the better part of my life being a mechanic, not a salesman. I've always had a burning desire to take things apart and understand how they work, rather than sell them to someone else.

I have extensive experience working in both domestic and foreign markets, plus solid knowledge of how options and synthetics work. I have also seen up close the investments carried on the balance sheets of pension funds and university endowments. Yet with all that insight into the investment world, I have always held my 401(k)—and my father's 401(k)—in passively managed and well-diversified Vanguard index funds.

It may seem odd that someone with my exposure to advanced investment tools and techniques would advocate a passive investing approach like Vanguard's index funds. But Vanguard is one of the best retail solutions on the market for the average investor as well as for the pragmatic, sophisticated investor. Incidentally, Vanguard funds are not sold by brokers, so the firm doesn't pay commissions. It also returns most of its profits back to its investors.

So, it may be no surprise to many of you that my two heroes in the investing world are John Bogle and Warren Buffett. Bogle, the founder of Vanguard, turned Wall Street upside down beginning in the 1970s by being a staunch advocate for the general investing public. His premise has always been very straightforward: to provide a powerful vehicle for very low-cost diversification.

My other hero, legendary investor Warren Buffett, lives by two important rules:

- Rule #1: Never lose money.
- Rule #2: Never forget rule #1.

At his core, Buffett is a "value guy." He invests in companies that make tangible things, and he invests in businesses that he can fully understand. Despite his brilliance and long-term track record of success, every investment decision that Buffett makes requires the agreement of his longtime partner, Charlie Munger.

Neither Buffett nor Munger has a corporate agenda. Both are advocates for people and their finances. Their principles are priceless, and they offer intelligent advice to the average investor.

> Rule #1: Never lose money.
>
> Rule #2: Never forget rule #1.
>
> Warren Buffett

My investment philosophy is now centered on an offshoot of Buffett and Bogle's philosophy. First, control what you can control—costs, risks and taxes. Second, rely on financial science to produce the results. We work with a group that I refer to as Vanguard 2.0. Its premise is to diversify investments across 10,000 stocks in a low-cost, tax-efficient manner. We're lucky to be partnered with what I believe to be the best institutional solution for our clients. As a result of the work and extensive research they have done, three of its board members have received Nobel Prizes in economics. My money and my family's money are invested with this group.

> First, control what you can control—costs, risks and taxes. Second, rely on financial science to produce the results.

A mechanic would tell you that to improve your odds of success with an older car, you need to change the oil every 3,000 miles and let the car warm up sufficiently before driving it. Do these recommendations guarantee that a car will always run perfectly? No, but they definitely increase the odds. When it comes to investing, I always want science and the odds to be on my side, my father's side, and my clients' side.

> One of the first cars I purchased was a 1987 BMW that had 100,000 miles on it. I followed the mechanic's practical advice and drove it to 200,000 miles. The last I heard from the next owner was that this vehicle has reached 275,000 miles. Find a good mechanic and listen.

INVESTING IS LIKE SURFING

As some of you may know, I'm passionate about surfing, despite growing up in the Midwest. Sometimes when surfing, you get pulled underwater by a big wave. The instinct is to fight the force of the wave, but what you really want to do is surrender to the power of the wave and know that if you do, you will eventually float back to the surface. You're at the mercy of the ocean, just like you're at the mercy of the market. You can't fight the market, but if you stay within your plan and don't panic when things get rough, in the end, you'll likely come out on top. In surfing, you can minimize the chance of being pulled underwater by using your head: Don't go out on days with big waves, or if you do, opt out of the very large ones. Investing is no different—you can minimize the chance of being pulled under by using your head.

> Investing is similar to surfing—you can minimize the chance of being pulled under by using your head.

As we help clients navigate their financial life, sometimes the most basic principles are all they need. No matter what, I love doing it. Many of the entrepreneurs we work with are philanthropically inclined. It's very gratifying to help them use their money to make a positive impact on the world.

My father always advised me to help people in life. I'm fortunate that I found a pathway to do that. Now in my 40s, I realize that my dad was right about a lot more things than I thought growing up.

C h a p t e r

ADDRESSING YOUR KEY FINANCIAL CHALLENGES AS YOU APPROACH A LIQUIDITY EVENT

K e y   T a k e a w a y s :

■ Proactive tax planning, implemented **before** a liquidity event occurs, can significantly reduce your tax bill—potentially saving you millions of dollars.

■ Don't leave money on the table by underestimating your value or by agreeing to a deal that doesn't maximize your wealth.

■ Protect your post-liquidity wealth. Two-thirds of successful business owners have been involved in unjust personal lawsuits and/or divorce proceedings.

As an entrepreneur, you have lots of peers. Currently, there are over 28 million businesses in the United States[1]—the highest number on record.

But as a highly successful entrepreneur preparing for a liquidity event, you are in much more exclusive company. Many of your colleagues—even successful, hardworking ones—never reach that golden destination of having a successful exit and realizing tremendous financial value for themselves and their families. Before you move further toward that goal, take a moment to reflect on your accomplishments to date and congratulate yourself on the impressive results of your efforts.

Now is also the time to take stock of the key financial challenges you must address as you approach a liquidity event. As is true for many entrepreneurs, the company you built (or run) is the single biggest asset on your personal balance sheet. That means you have a number of issues to consider before, during and after the sale of your business. More than likely, the vast majority of your time and energy has been spent working on the day-to-day operations of your business. You probably haven't had the opportunity or inclination to think carefully about your exit strategy.

If you take the time now to formulate the right strategies, you will find that the liquidity event process can be a smooth ride. With the right advanced planning, you will be able to maximize your personal wealth—and do so on your own terms. By identifying the key financial challenges you face and by approaching them strategically, you will put yourself in the best possible position to accomplish three important objectives:

1. Maximize the wealth you receive through a liquidity event or exit.

2. Preserve that wealth for generations, if desired.

3. Achieve both the success and peace of mind that you envision for yourself, your family and your community.

If you don't take the time to get your financial house in order, you can quickly find yourself eroding the value of your personal balance sheet that you have worked so hard to build—and potentially suffering from a range of negative financial and emotional outcomes. With that in mind, this chapter examines five key financial considerations to address as you near a liquidity event.

LIQUIDITY EVENTS: AN OVERVIEW

First, the following is an overview of the various types of liquidity events and exit strategies that successful entrepreneurs tend to take:

1. Initial public offering (IPO).

2. Sale to a private third party (private equity firm, private competitor).

3. Internal sale to one or more partners, the existing management team or employee(s).

4. Acquisition by a public company.

5. Partial sale (aka "taking a bite of the apple")—

selling a partial stake to achieve liquidity while still being involved in the business and retaining some ownership.

It is important to note that each of these options, when employed properly, can help you achieve your liquidity goals and can give you the financial freedom to transition successfully to the next stage of your life. The key is to identify and use the option that is best suited for you and your situation. The good news: There are numerous resources available to help you do that analysis. For example, we introduce entrepreneurs to helpful experts with whom we have longstanding relationships, such as investment bankers, business brokers, M&A attorneys, private equity firms and venture capitalists, and even a financial therapist to help you navigate the psychological components.

> Three important objectives:
> 1. Maximize the wealth you receive through a liquidity event or exit.
> 2. Preserve that wealth for generations, if desired.
> 3. Achieve both the success and peace of mind that you envision for yourself, your family and your community.

THE FIVE KEY FINANCIAL CHALLENGES

Based on my years of experience helping successful entrepreneurs, as well as my research and interviews with experts in the area of successful business exits, I have identified five key financial challenges that entrepreneurs who are about to "cash out" must address. The idea is to ensure that you make a smooth and successful transition from where you are today to where you want to be post-exit.

1. Minimizing income taxes on the transaction. It's vital to determine the likely tax exposure that a liquidity event will trigger for you. You'll also want to avoid any unpleasant tax surprises and mitigate that tax bill as much as possible.

Proactive tax planning that is implemented **before** your transaction can significantly reduce your tax bill. By how much? Consider that without a plan, you can pay more than 50 percent of your earnings in taxes here in California.[2] If you take a few basic steps, you can reduce that tax burden to around 37 percent. And if you make all the right moves in advance of the transaction, your tax bill can fall below 30 percent. Many entrepreneurs miss the "QSSB" rule that could potentially eliminate 100 percent of the taxes paid. Advanced planning can result in millions of dollars in taxes saved.

Despite the significant impact that tax planning can have on their net worth, entrepreneurs too often fail to plan around taxes effectively or don't plan effectively enough. This should be at the top of your mind as you move toward liquidity. Perhaps most important, the discussions you have about tax planning need to be with professionals who deeply understand the situations and unique issues that you face as an entrepreneur. There are more than 77,000 pages in the U.S. tax code, and the rules and regulations pertaining to liquidity events are among the most complex on the books.

To have a successful liquidity event, you'll probably need to go beyond a standard planning session with an accountant. You'll want to engage with a specialized CPA firm, plus a law firm that works with entrepreneurs that are approaching liquidity events, as well as other specialists such as derivative and valuation experts. With expert strategies, you'll find smarter ways to maximize your wealth and ensure ideal outcomes for yourself and your family. For example, if you have stock options, you can take steps to "get the clock ticking" on those options as early as possible. That way, gains from the sale can be treated as long-term capital gains instead of as short-term gains, thus potentially cutting your tax bill in half.

2. Maximizing wealth by not "leaving money on the table." To get where you are today, you have had to make many smart decisions along the way. Your expertise about your business and your entire industry may be unmatched by anyone else. However, a liquidity event is a different beast entirely. There are numerous ways that you can unwillingly leave money on the table.

Say, for example, that you are a business owner selling your company to a private equity firm. Your job—your life—is to be great at your business. But the job of the

MBAs sitting across the table from you is to acquire companies at an attractive price. Most likely they simply know the world of acquisitions better than you do. Your business might be selling software; their business is buying businesses.

This imbalance can leave you feeling uncertain, or even fearful that you are not getting a deal that maximizes your value creation. At best, without proper planning, you'll leave some money on the table. In extreme cases, transactions can fall apart entirely because the deal terms include risks that the business owners don't fully appreciate.

During my research, I interviewed many entrepreneurs who had successful exits from the businesses they ran. One of the questions I always ask is "What is your biggest regret?" Surprisingly (or not), some say exiting their business was their biggest regret. Others say their biggest mistake was agreeing to a cap on the earn-out. By underestimating their own value, they ended up leaving a lot of money on the table.

I've discussed failure with entrepreneurs. In one case, a private equity firm came in with an attractive offer for the founder's company. One of the terms was that the private equity firm would infuse capital in the short term, ramp up the company's staff and incur additional overhead to lay the groundwork for expansion. However, neither the founder nor the private equity firm anticipated the dramatic shift in the economy that occurred in 2008. The severe recession caused the deal to fall apart and the business ultimately folded, largely because of the ill-timed expansion plans.

3. Preserving wealth by avoiding excessive single-stock risk. If you are getting acquired by a publicly traded company, the deal may be done entirely by using the acquiring company's stock. That means post-deal, the lion's share of your wealth will be in just one stock—the acquiring company's—and you will be incurring tremendous single-company risk from your lack of diversification.

The fact is, companies can—and do—blow up unexpectedly. (Remember Fannie Mae and Freddie Mac, "government-sponsored entities" that lost over 90 percent of their value?) By keeping the majority of your money in the shares of just one company, you risk losing enormous wealth in short order. Having lived through the dot-com bust in San Francisco, I unfortunately witnessed several instances. Take for example these dot-com darlings that crashed back to earth:

	High Stock Price	Low Stock Price	Pct. of Wealth Lost
Pets.com	$11	$1	90%
Webvan	$30	$.06	99%
eToys	$84	$.01 +/-	99%

One of the saddest examples of single-company risk occurred when media mogul Ted Turner lost $8 billion that he had concentrated in the stock of AOL Time Warner. While he was still a billionaire, the AOL Time Warner implosion had a devastating effect on Turner, his family and many of the philanthropic causes his family supported.

That said, addressing single-stock risk or single-company risk can be challenging. For one, you are "on the inside" in your industry, which gives you justifiable confidence. This can be especially true if your company is acquired by an industry competitor. This can lead to a false sense of security and knowledge about the future of the company and its stock. You may think you know the industry backward and forward, and would be able to sense if something was about to go wrong. This knowledge might have been useful when the company was still private. However, once a firm becomes part of a publicly traded operation, insider information can no longer be used to benefit yourself or anyone you know financially. Even if you do have knowledge of impending negative news, you might not be able to share it, much less do anything about it. It's at times like these that you then begin to gamble with your financial health.

Even very financially astute entrepreneurs can fall into the trap of being overly concentrated in a single stock. For years, you've been used to having the bulk of your wealth tied up in just one place—your company. So after going through an exit or liquidity event, having most of your wealth concentrated in just a single stock can seem perfectly natural. That's especially true if the stock of the acquiring firm is red-hot. You don't want to miss out on the gains if you sell or even trim back your holdings.

There is also a social-emotional issue at work here, as some entrepreneurs worry that they might appear to be disloyal or that they are "going against the team" by selling some of the shares they hold of the acquiring company's stock.

So, is the solution to diversify by holding many, many stocks? No. Major stock market corrections punish even the best of companies. Instead, we recommend a broadly diversified portfolio of assets including fixed income, real estate, private equity, limited partnerships and investments in companies that you own and have control over.

The bottom line: Preserve your own wealth and let the gamblers gamble with theirs.

4. Transferring wealth effectively and tax-efficiently.
In the wake of a liquidity event, it is possible—even likely—that your own financial needs are well in hand. Once that is the case, you may be looking to ensure that your parents, children and grandchildren are well taken care of—and in accordance with your wishes and stipulations.

Transferring wealth through estate planning requires you to decide how your assets will be distributed when you're gone. This means determining how and when your heirs will receive money or business interests, and ensuring that the maximum amount possible is transferred to heirs while minimizing taxes. Proper estate planning is the most effective way to ensure that you can leave a legacy for your loved ones in a way that satisfies your wishes and provides for the financial health and well-being of your family. You may be familiar with the stress that so often comes with multiple family members attempting to sort out a single estate. The idea is to lessen the chances of, and if possible prevent, that situation from occurring.

The bottom line: Preserve your own wealth and let the gamblers gamble with theirs.

Estate planning is one of the most important, yet misunderstood, areas of entrepreneurs' financial lives. Estate taxes, for example, usually receive all the attention, and it's easy to see why: If they are not properly addressed, the government can grab 40 percent of what you worked so hard to build.

That said, taxes are only one part of a broader estate planning picture. You also need to focus on issues such as management and wealth succession concerns, selection of successor managers or trustees, and preparing your loved ones to receive and make the best use of the money they will eventually inherit.

Estate planning can become especially important prior to a liquidity event that results in you having significantly more money than you ever had in the past. Yesterday, an estate plan may have been the last thing on your mind. Today, it becomes your top priority. Even if you have a thorough estate plan in place, going through a liquidity event will create dramatic changes to your personal balance sheet and will limit the potential advanced planning opportunities available to you now.

In short, estate planning is not a "one and done" exercise. The best estate plans are dynamic, living strategies that can be—and should be—adapted and optimized to reflect the changes that inevitably occur over the course of your life.

5. Protecting your money from being taken unjustly.
Guarding your newly acquired wealth against potential creditors, lawsuits, children's spouses, potential ex-spouses and catastrophic loss should be a key consideration. By historical standards, the number of lawsuits against the affluent in recent years is high. Yet entrepreneurs rarely focus enough on protecting themselves. Consider these sobering statistics from Prince Associates:

- Approximately 65 percent of successful business owners[3] said they have been involved in unjust personal lawsuits and/or divorce proceedings.

- Roughly 90 percent of these business owners said they are concerned about such lawsuits.

- Only about one in four business owners (26.9 percent) has a plan in place to protect his or her assets.

Wealth protection strategies can be used to help safeguard your wealth so that your assets are not unjustly taken—and so you can enjoy greater peace of mind knowing that your financial security is indeed secure. How you address these concerns will depend on your specific situation. But common actions include controlling risks though restructuring various assets and considering legal forms of ownership—trusts, limited liability entities and so on—that put a shield between your money and other parties that might not have your best interest in mind.

It's critical to realize, however, that for asset protection strategies to be effective and able to withstand legal challenges, they must be put in place well before they are actually needed. The upshot: You need to plot out an asset protection plan sooner rather than later if you want to truly guard the significant wealth you now have (or are about to have).

CREATING A STRATEGY

As you review these five key challenges above, reflect on

your own situation. Chances are you share some of these concerns in your life—perhaps all of them. Or maybe these are issues that you haven't given much thought to in the past, and you're now a bit closer to seeing how crucial it is to create a strategy that tackles them head-on.

Your response to these challenges—and others you might face—will be an enormous driver of the level of financial success and peace of mind that you seek as you move toward liquidity. In the next chapter, you will learn about a framework for financial decision making that will help you build a truly comprehensive plan for managing the full spectrum of your money—today, tomorrow and for decades to come.

Chapter

2

COLLABORATIVE WEALTH MANAGEMENT: THE RIGHT FRAMEWORK FOR ACHIEVING FINANCIAL SUCCESS

Key Takeaways:

■ Collaborative Wealth Management is designed to solve your full range of challenges and to coordinate all aspects of your financial life.

■ The advanced planning component of Collaborative Wealth Management addresses tax mitigation, wealth transfer, asset protection, charitable giving and next-stage life planning.

■ Part of your job as your family's CEO is to find someone who can provide collaborative financial guidance by serving as your family's *Personal CFO*.

You have now identified many of the key challenges that you and your family must address on your journey to financial success and freedom. It will take hard work, discipline and smart thinking to overcome and solve those challenges. Nothing truly valuable is free or easy, and a lifetime of financial peace of mind is no different.

The good news: You don't have to do it yourself. As a hard-driving entrepreneur, you might be surprised to hear that. But in this case, you have help that can empower you to close the gap between where you are today and where you want to be down the road.

That help is a process called **Collaborative Wealth Management**, and it is designed to help entrepreneurs get their financial lives on the right track—and stay there.

Wealth management means having *all* of your financial challenges addressed and your entire financial situation enhanced. Collaborative Wealth Management goes beyond traditional investment solutions and addresses a wide variety of financial needs that you have throughout the many and varied phases of your life—including before and after you experience a liquidity event. True Collaborative Wealth Management enables you to organize and manage your money so that all the components of your financial life work together toward one purpose—achieving the goals you most want for yourself, your family, your community and the world at large.

"WEALTH MANAGEMENT" DEFINED
The phrase "wealth management" is one you are likely to

hear time and time again as you seek advice about your financial challenges and opportunities.

But as you will come to see, just because someone says they provide wealth management services doesn't necessarily mean they can actually deliver. Ask 10 "wealth managers" to define wealth management. You're likely to get 10 different answers—and most will be heavily focused on the standard investment management services that everyone else provides. In most cases, these standard services are not enough to make a meaningful difference in your total financial picture.

True Collaborative Wealth Management is designed to solve a full range of challenges that affluent entrepreneurs face on an ongoing, long-term basis. Most importantly, Collaborative Wealth Management coordinates all aspects of your financial life that must be addressed if you are to build a secure and meaningful future.

It accomplishes this in three ways:

1. Using a collaborative process to gain a detailed understanding of your deepest values, goals, and most important financial wants and needs. A collaborative approach allows a wealth manager to clarify what is most important to you and craft a long-range and measurable wealth management plan designed to meet those needs and goals. The process is designed to foster an ongoing and dynamic relationship with you to ensure your needs continue to be met as they change over time.

2. Going beyond basic investments to use customized solutions to fit your unique needs and goals beyond simply investments. The range of interrelated financial services and tools might include, for example, investment management, advanced retirement planning, insurance, estate planning, business and exit planning, pre-liquidity planning, charitable gifting, and wealth protection.

Collaborative Wealth Management is designed to solve a full range of challenges that affluent entrepreneurs face on an ongoing, long-term basis. Most importantly, Collaborative Wealth Management coordinates all aspects of your financial life that must be addressed if you are to build a secure and meaningful future.

3. Implementing these customized solutions in close consultation with your other professional advisors. Wealth management enables you and your professional wealth manager, if you work with one, to coordinate efforts closely with other trusted advisors (as desired) on an ongoing basis to identify your specific needs, and to design custom solutions to help meet those needs.

THE THREE KEY COMPONENTS OF TRUE COLLABORATIVE WEALTH MANAGEMENT

Wealth management consists of three key components, summed up in the following formula, that specifically address and solve the most pressing financial challenges you face:

Wealth Management (WM) = Investment Consulting (IC) + Advanced Planning (AP) + Relationship Management (RM)

1. Investment consulting (IC). This deals with the overarching concern shared by all successful entrepreneurs and their families: making consistent, smart decisions about their finances. Investment consulting aligns your financial assets to your goals, return objectives, time horizons and risk tolerance. It is the foundation upon which a true **Collaborative Wealth Management** solution is created.

Through investment consulting, you can address what is perhaps the most pressing specific financial issue you face as a successful entrepreneur—wealth preservation. You want to keep the money that you have worked hard to earn.

The key investment planning concepts that you can use to guide the management of your investment portfolios will be explored in Chapter 3.

2. Advanced planning (AP). This component addresses a broad range of important financial needs in five key areas that go *beyond* investments.

i) **Mitigating taxes:** Enhancing wealth by, among other things, reducing the impact of taxes on your bottom line and decreasing borrowing costs.

ii) **Transferring wealth:** Determining how your

money can best support your children, grandchildren and other family members, as well as causes you care about, while minimizing the tax paid to the government.

iii) **Ensuring that your assets are not unjustly taken:** Protecting the money you have earned by safeguarding it from creditors, lawsuits and other parties that could seek to possess your assets.

iv) **Maximizing charitable giving and planning:** Leveraging your money to magnify the impact you can have on your community and on society at large.

v) **Defining the next chapter of your life:** Remaining relevant and engaged, and having a purpose.

These non-investment-related concerns are hugely important to your long-term financial success. Yet they are often overlooked or viewed (incorrectly) as secondary concerns— even by financial professionals. Indeed, research indicates that a mere 6 percent of financial advisors deal with their clients' advanced planning issues. Therefore, very few investors address these five concerns in any systematic, comprehensive manner. For these reasons, the five main areas of advanced planning will be discussed in detail in Chapter 4.

3. Relationship management (RM) is the third and final component. It involves meeting your investment and advanced planning needs over time by assembling and working with a team of financial and related professionals in a coordinated manner. The expert who can help you the most depends on your unique situation: This team of experts could include attorneys, accountants, business consultants, valuation and risk specialists, and even a financial therapist. Relationship management is a key part of building and maintaining a Collaborative Wealth Management process. When done right, it can provide you with a full range of expertise that's built to address the complexities of your wealth, and can coordinate the efforts of those experts so that all your strategies work in concert with each other for optimal outcomes. Relationship management will be reviewed more closely in Chapter 5.

A true Collaborative Wealth Management approach is process-driven: It is highly defined and consists of very specific steps. In seeking out the best advisor for you, try to keep the three key components of investment consulting, advanced planning and relationship management in mind. Ask questions. If the plan you're being offered does not integrate all three, it probably won't have the impact that you're seeking.

THE WEALTH MANAGEMENT PROCESS

proc·ess1

ˈpräˌses,ˈprōˌses/

Noun

1. a series of actions or steps taken in order to achieve a
   particular end.

We believe the right framework is a prerequisite to success. The Collaborative Wealth Management approach consists of a series of five meetings. These meetings will help you identify your unique and specific challenges as well as design and implement a range of tailored solutions.

The Collaborative Wealth Management Process

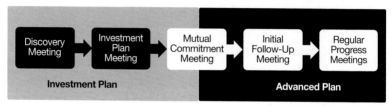

Discovery Meeting → Investment Plan Meeting → Mutual Commitment Meeting → Initial Follow-Up Meeting → Regular Progress Meetings

Investment Plan | **Advanced Plan**

1. The Mutual Discovery Meeting. The first step is to help you accurately uncover and clearly measure what you want and need most out of life today and in the future. Without knowing what you want your money to accomplish, even the best financial strategies in the world won't be of much help.

With that in mind, the initial Mutual Discovery Meeting is centered on a detailed interview process that enables you to define your financial needs and goals, and where you are currently in life. This gives you the information you need to create your comprehensive profile (more on that below). This profile is used to create solutions that are customized to your situation, and to lay the groundwork required for working with other advisors (CPAs, attorneys, risk specialists, etc.) who may be involved in the wealth management process.

Because this part of the process is so critical to your success—and because few investors ever do a formal Mutual Discovery Meeting interview—we focus extra attention on this step below.

2. The Investment Plan Meeting. This meeting is centered on two key elements.

1. A complete diagnostic overview of your current financial situation.

2. Presentation of a recommended plan and policy statement for achieving your investment-related goals.

These elements are based on the information that was uncovered during the Mutual Discovery Meeting. These recommendations are based on the four key drivers of investment success: **return, risk, costs and taxes**. The plan presented in this meeting becomes your actionable investment plan, which is structured to accomplish two main goals:

1. Bridge any gaps between where you are and where you want to be.

2. Maximize the probability of achieving your well-defined investment goals.

In short, the investment plan serves as the road map that will guide you through the journey of growing, preserving and passing on your wealth over time. Having a plan in place will help ensure that rational analysis—not emotional reaction—is the basis for your investment decisions.

3. The Mutual Commitment Meeting. Before committing to a wealth management investment plan, make sure you consider it very thoroughly. At this meeting, which occurs after you have reviewed the plan carefully, you go over any questions or concerns you have about the plan to determine whether to move ahead and implement the recommended investment strategies. Upon your approval, the investment plan is put into motion. You'll decide on the frequency of your future meetings with your advisor and the ways in which you prefer to be contacted.

4. The 45-Day Follow-up Meeting. Within 45 days of implementing your investment plan, you will receive a great deal of legally required paperwork. You're busy, and you may find all these forms and emails a bit of a nuisance. This meeting helps you organize the various statements you have received. It also allows a wealth manager to help you understand the financial paperwork involved in working together. And it's an opportunity to review any initial concerns and ask any questions you have. It's an opportunity to gain continued clarity about exactly what the plan is for preserving your wealth.

5. Regular Progress Meetings. The creation of a wealth management plan is not a "one and done" exercise. It's an ongoing process. Over time, the markets change and, more important, our lives change—especially in the wake of a sizable liquidity event. It's important to review and update your plan consistently. At Regular Progress Meetings, your current financial position is compared to your plan to assess the progress you have made toward your goals.

Included in this plan is a strategy for addressing your critical *non-investment* goals. This comprehensive blueprint for addressing your advanced planning needs will be developed in coordination with a network of professionals such as CPAs and attorneys. At subsequent Progress Meetings, you can decide how to proceed on specific elements of the wealth management plan. Over time, every aspect of your complete financial picture can be effectively managed.

THE KEY ROLE OF THE PERSONAL CFO

As you have probably realized by now, truly consultative and Collaborative Wealth Management stands in stark contrast to how most investors operate today. Even the most affluent among us rarely take this type of coordinated and comprehensive approach with their finances. The vast majority tend to address financial needs and goals like retirement and estate planning on an ad hoc basis—treating these issues as separate concerns and placing each one in its own discrete box. Given that, their efforts to deal with their many interconnected issues are not coordinated.

This leads to challenges that can jeopardize their financial health as well as that of their families and their businesses. This is why it's so important to manage wealth comprehensively: It lets you see the big picture at all times and manage your finances around the whole instead of focusing on only one aspect.

Unfortunately, many financial advisors and other professionals also take an ad hoc, rather than comprehensive, approach to wealth management. They deal with issues only when they arise, and gather just enough information to implement a single particular response to the current problem at hand. As noted earlier, many financial firms these days claim that they offer comprehensive wealth management, but in reality they focus almost exclusively on investment management. They may offer a few additional services, but they lack the truly comprehensive approach that you need to coordinate your entire financial life.

To make wealth management a true part of your financial life, you need to recognize an important fact—one that you'll no doubt appreciate:

You are not just the CEO of a company—you are the CEO of your family.

Being the CEO of your family (or the co-CEO, along with your spouse or partner) means that you have a duty to define a vision for your family. Think about what you truly value and what

> You are not just the CEO of a company—you are the CEO of your family.

you want to achieve together. Then you can better determine the best path to make that vision a reality—just as you would define your firm's direction and path.

Part of your responsibility as the wise CEO of your family is deciding where you may want to get specialized help with regard to your journey toward realizing your vision. The most common area in which "family CEOs" look for guidance is their finances. That's why it's so important to find someone who can take on the role of your family's *personal CFO*.

In some ways, the financial side of your family unit is actually a lot like the financial side of your business. In both cases, there are important decisions to be made about spending, saving, investing and planning for future growth and preservation. And as with any business, you and your family need a financial leader who can present you with good ideas, act as a sounding board and work with you to ensure that you have what you need to make smart decisions about your money—just as the CFO at your company does.

Some CEOs of their families choose to double as their families' CFOs—committing to thinking through the full range of financial challenges they face and developing optimal responses that work in concert with each other. Others choose to find a trusted financial professional, such as a wealth manager, who can act as a personal CFO for the family, and work with them collaboratively. This is a decision that you must make consciously and carefully, based on your ability and willingness to be a successful CFO for your family. But whether you act on your own or work in partnership with a professional, by using a Collaborative Wealth Management process, you will give yourself a tremendous advantage over investors who take a more simplistic approach to managing their financial lives.

SPOTLIGHT ON THE MUTUAL DISCOVERY MEETING AND TOTAL INVESTOR PROFILE

Part of what makes wealth management so effective in addressing entrepreneurs' needs is the Mutual Discovery Meeting. This initial stage of the process focuses on helping you identify your deepest, most important financial wants and needs.

The reason for this is simple: It's only after those needs and wants are identified that a customized portfolio can be designed to support those goals. Without this foundational information, the management of wealth becomes nebulous and ill-defined. You can't solve the complex and sometimes conflicting challenges you face until you position your assets around the values, needs, goals and issues that are most important to you *as a person*.

The Mutual Discovery Meeting helps you identify all that is most important to you in **seven key areas of your life**. Your answers to the types of Mutual Discovery Meeting questions shown below will help develop an all-encompassing picture of who you are and what you want from life so that your assets can be positioned to support you accordingly.

1) Values. What is truly important to you about your money and your desire for success, and what are the key, deep-seated values underlying the decisions you make to attain them? When you think about your money, what concerns, needs or feelings come to mind?

This is a particularly important area to address. Our values are core motivators of everything we do in our lives. They have a profound impact on every important decision we make. And yet, most of us have trouble articulating our values. Even entrepreneurs who may have carefully spelled out the core values of their businesses often have not done a "deep dive" into their personal values. The Mutual Discovery Meeting interview process can therefore bring substantial advantages to the process of managing your wealth effectively.

2) Goals. What do you want to achieve with your money over the long run? Think professionally and personally, from the most practical to your biggest dream.

3) Relationships. Which people in your life are most

important to you? Think family, employees, friends and colleagues (and even your pets if they're considered part of your family).

4) Assets. What do you own? Where and how are your assets held? From your business assets to real estate to investment accounts, artwork and retirement plans, it's important to take stock of it all.

5) Advisors. On whom do you rely for advice? How do you feel about the professional relationships you currently have? Wealth management is designed to work in partnership with all of your trusted advisors to arrive at customized, comprehensive solutions that complement each other.

6) Process. How actively do you like to be involved in managing your financial life? How do you prefer to work with your trusted advisors?

7) Interests. What are your passions in life? Consider your hobbies, favorite sports and leisure activities, charitable and philanthropic involvements, and religious and spiritual relationships, as well as your children's schools and activities.

Your answers to these questions are used to create your Investor Profile, which will serve as a road map for ensuring that every financial decision you make supports what you want most from life (see the following chart below).

Your Investor Profile

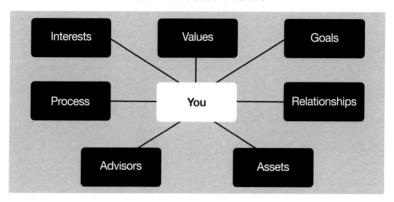

If, like most affluent entrepreneurs, you currently work with one or more financial advisors, you are probably aware that most professionals use some type of fact-finding process when first meeting with their clients or prospects.

But have you ever noticed that these questions usually focus almost exclusively on your assets and your net worth? In contrast, note that only one of the seven categories that make up Collaborative Wealth Management's Investor Profile concerns financial assets. Six of the seven are focused on helping you (and your wealth manager, if you use one) better understand who you are *as a person*.

There's a big advantage to getting at this information. By engaging in this mutual discovery process and using the insight you gain to create a personalized profile, your wealth and all the choices you make involving it become better aligned with the life you want to build.

A CLOSER LOOK

Of course, this is just a high-level overview of the Collaborative Wealth Management process. The following three chapters will explore, in greater detail, each main component of wealth management.

- Investment consulting
- Advanced planning
- Relationship management

These chapters will show you how Collaborative Wealth Management is a process-driven approach to positioning your wealth. It's designed to help you achieve all that is truly most important to you, your family and your community.

GIVING CREDIT WHERE CREDIT IS DUE

I would like to think that I am exceptionally brilliant and came up with the wealth management formula on my own. In reality, I've had a great deal of guidance from some incredible mentors. We had our own version of a wealth management formula in the early days of our firm. It was this: **"What's the best possible way to help our clients solve problems and make their lives easier? And if we can't solve it (often that is the case), we will find a professional that can."**

We still operate that way today, but a couple of fine gentlemen have provided us with a well-defined process born out of years of research and working for decades with the Super Rich, those defined as having a net worth of $500 million or more. This "process" and "definition" are adopted and executed by only about 6 percent of advisors.

Chapter

INVESTMENT CONSULTING: THE FOUNDATION OF A COLLABORATIVE WEALTH MANAGEMENT PLAN

Key Takeaways:

- Post-liquidity event, it's crucial to focus on preserving wealth. This may require you to adopt a new mindset about your money, investing and risk.

- Asset allocation decisions are crucial. They will drive your long-term investment results more than any other factor will.

- Consistently owning a wide variety of assets— including global stocks and bonds—can help you better protect *and* grow your wealth over time.

Having realized significant wealth through a liquidity event, or if you're soon about to do so, you may suddenly find it quite easy to finance your current goals, desires and objectives. An entrepreneur in your situation might have more money than it seems like you'll ever really *need*—perhaps a lot more.

Although that could be true objectively, it doesn't always feel that way. Even if you're more than comfortable now financially, you may still worry about having enough money to maintain your lifestyle in the long run. You're not interested in limiting yourself, and perhaps you simply do not subscribe to the "I've got all I need" mentality. You have spent a lifetime seeking to build, create and have *more*. That desire may be a key component of what makes you *you*.

That said, your money *does* put you in a unique position as an investor. Unlike the majority of people who invest in pursuit of maximum growth, you do not need to look to the financial markets or alternative investment opportunities to make your money. You've already done that through your business.

It's now time to focus on *preserving* the money you have earned. Yes, growth may still be one of your financial objectives, but it doesn't necessarily belong at the top of your list. The biggest financial priority for you and your family now is to manage your finances intelligently so you don't lose what you have worked so hard to build. In this chapter, we'll look at what it means to make the smartest possible investment decisions in the wake of a liquidity event.

RETHINKING INVESTMENT RISK, POST-LIQUIDITY

"The way to become rich is to put all your eggs in one basket and then watch that basket." —Andrew Carnegie

That quote from Andrew Carnegie will certainly ring true for you as a successful entrepreneur. Your laser-like focus on one basket—your company—is what got you to where you are today.

But going forward, the approach that served you so well as a business owner is probably not the best method for taking care of the wealth that you have already realized.

My team and I believe that wealth preservation should now be your primary concern. Consider that nearly nine out of 10 affluent individuals (88 percent) say that "losing their wealth" is a major concern.

If you can successfully preserve your wealth, you can maintain your lifestyle, help your family and leave a legacy—while avoiding financial mistakes along the way.

But, as with many others who have gone through a liquidity event, the idea of investing to preserve wealth may require you to adopt a fundamentally different mindset.

OK, SO WHERE DO I START?

It's easy to see why the concept of *preservation* may be out of sync with your preferences and innate tendencies.

As a successful business owner, you've probably been quite comfortable over the years taking risks—it's served you well, and you may even see risk-taking as essential to generating results in business and in the capital markets.

Even if you now find yourself with more money than you'll ever be able to spend—and therefore have no practical reason to take on significant investment risk—you may find yourself drawn to "opportunities" that carry with them a sizable probability of losing most, if not all, of your investment. It's part of your DNA.

Your reason for pursuing these investments may be to continue to grow your bottom line. But pursuing risky investments is not always about making more money. For many in your position, the money is secondary to the thrill of the challenge, the hunt or the competition. Mark Cuban, the internet billionaire and owner of the NBA's Dallas Mavericks, speaks frequently about being unable to turn off his competitive engine. It can be very difficult to disengage from risk-prone behavior in favor of placing your assets in "boring" strategies.

When it comes to wealth preservation, your propensity to take risks can become a serious issue.

WHAT IF I CAN AFFORD THE RISK?

Even if you now can afford to lose significant sums in pursuit of huge investment payoffs, or even if you are in a position to "spin the wheel" without being impacted too severely by poor outcomes, it's simply not the smart move. Taking these risks can erode your ability to make a major difference with your money later on—for example, by taking care of multiple generations of family members or by contributing to philanthropic organizations whose values match yours.

Your historical experience with uncertainty might also cause you to take on more investment risk than you realize you're taking—or intend to take. It is extremely common for successful individuals and families to reach retirement age with 70 percent or more of their investable assets in stocks. With a closer look, it becomes clear that such investment positioning is often far more aggressive than it needs to be. Instead, their risk allocation should be *based on what truly matters to them*.

Consider the example of a physician who owned a lucrative independent medical practice. Through his work, he learned a lot about pharmaceutical companies. He became so enamored of one company in particular that he allocated his entire pool of investable assets to the company's stock. When I met with the physician, his stake had lost 50 percent of its value—and in my last discussion with him, he used the word "hope" when talking about his investment strategy. *If there's one thing you take away from this story, remember that "hope" is not a strategy.*

This example may seem extreme—but it's not uncommon. I have seen hasty

decisions and poor advice lead to excessive stock concentration in failed investments like Enron, Bear Sterns, Lehman Brothers, Countrywide, Fannie Mae—the list goes on. These decisions have resulted in actual permanent loss and, in the most extreme case, the individual having to return to work because of the heavy concentration in a single failed stock.

The worst part: Not one of these investors needed to incur so much risk in order to maintain their lifestyle. In fact, they weren't even aware of the amount of risk they were exposed to until it was too late.

Ultimately, there are two opposing forces at work as you seek to build a post-liquidity investment portfolio: the entrepreneurial risk-taker who measures success in terms of the amount of growth generated, and the investor who desires to preserve what's been built so it can be used for maximum benefit.

Essentially, this is every investor's dilemma—to balance risk and return. As we noted

Essentially, this is every investor's dilemma—to balance risk and return.

earlier, **we believe that wealth preservation should be the primary post-liquidity concern of successful entrepreneurs.**

SO IF I CAN'T INVEST MY MONEY IN SINGULAR CAUSES, HOW CAN I INVEST IT?

You may find yourself continually drawn to high-risk investing. If so, we encourage you to fill this need through other outlets—in other words, invest your time instead of your money. There's a lot to be gained by pursuing visceral hobbies, offering your expertise to friends in business and engaging in strategic problem solving for philanthropic organizations. Conversely, you might earmark a small portion of your assets for a personal investment or "venture fund" so you can pursue your interests without risking any life-altering losses. It's important to continue to support your investment in yourself and in your business. I have always been a firm believer that the best investment entrepreneurs will ever make is in themselves. No one knows your company, or yourself, like you do.

POTHOLES ON WALL STREET

"Compound interest is the eighth wonder of the world. He who understands it, earns it…he who doesn't…pays it." —Albert Einstein

Investing can be difficult. In one sense, we have every advantage over the long term to be properly compensated for the risk we take and to enjoy having the power of compounding on our side.

> Compound interest is the eighth wonder of the world. He who understands it, earns it…he who doesn't… pays it.
>
> Albert Einstein

Along the way, however, we face tremendous obstacles in the form of our emotions, the media and Wall Street-based attempts to sell us the hottest new ideas and strategies. I refer to these obstacles collectively as the potholes on Wall Street.

Consider the following headlines from 2007 when the stock market was establishing one of the most significant peaks in history (and right before everything crashed):

> *"Stocks are on track for solid gains…there's limited downside risk in the U.S. stock market from current levels."* (Hedge fund superstar Leon Cooperman, *Fortune*, August 8, 2007)

> *"Dow soars past 14,000 to register new all-time high, buoyed by belief that the worst of the credit crisis has passed."* (CNBC, October 2, 2007)

> *"The impact on the broader economy and financial markets of the problems in the subprime market seems likely to be contained."* (Ben Bernanke, March 2007)

> *"We expect a return to a more normal earnings environment."* (Chuck Prince, Citibank, October 2007)

Two years later, with the financial crisis fresh in our memories, the market was at it again as it fell to a bottom of historic proportions. Here were some accompanying headlines:

"We believe that 2009 will be tougher than many anticipated.... The world's first global recession is just getting started." (Ian Bremmer and Nouriel Roubini, *Wall Street Journal*, January 23, 2009)

"It's way too early to get back into U.S. stocks.... Expect meltdowns in securities backed by credit card debt, home equity, student and auto loans as well as commercial real estate." (Gary A. Shilling, "Field Day for Short-Sellers," *Forbes*, February 16, 2009)

"No End in Sight for Equities' Bear Hug." (*Financial Times*, February 25, 2009)

"Dow 5000? There's a Case for It." (*Wall Street Journal*, March 9, 2009)

...NONE OF THAT SOUNDS ACCURATE. HOW DO THE EXPERTS NAVIGATE ALL THIS?

Most often, they don't. Six years later the S&P 500 had returned more than 300 percent, more than tripling from its bottom set in March 2009. Bond returns were equally perplexing. It was the consensus view among amateurs and pros alike that interest rates would only go higher as the economic recovery progressed. Yet rates remain historically low and bonds have performed just fine (to everyone's surprise). Most of what we see and hear is just noise, but we have a difficult time avoiding it. In light of the current environment, it helps to tune in to a few consistent voices of reason and experience. Sober veterans like Berkshire Hathaway's Warren Buffett and Vanguard's John Bogle "keep it simple" when that is all that's required. Neither Buffett nor Bogle believes in, or even trusts, Wall Street. Bogle created a way for the average person to invest directly in the market. And Buffett has gone on record as saying that once he passes away, his money will be invested in the simplest way possible.

Markets are driven by fear and greed. The media is driven by headlines and provocative stories. Sadly, the majority of financial news (both on television and in print) is designed to "sell" stories rather than to inform and educate. Maybe this isn't surprising, but it's often forgotten. The media is a powerful force.

Later in this chapter we look at how the average investor's performance compares to the overall market. But what about the pros on Wall Street? Well, they have a very high bar: Turnover, fees, evaluations based on quarterly results, and the pressure of having to predict the market in the short term are all tough. But they are professionals on Wall Street—in the know and very smart. How do they fare against the S&P 500? As the table below shows, not very well.

	Equity Funds (managed)	S&P 500	$100K Compounded in Equity Funds	$100K Compounded in the S&P 500
20-Year	4.67%	8.19%	$249,141	$482,772
10-Year	4.23%	7.31%	$151,331	$202,489

Returns are for the period ending December 31, 2015. Average equity investor, average bond investor and average asset allocation investor performance results are calculated using data supplied by the Investment Company Institute. Investor returns are represented by the change in total mutual fund assets after excluding sales, redemptions and exchanges. This method of calculation captures realized and unrealized capital gains, dividends, interest, trading costs, sales charges, fees, expenses and any other costs. After calculating investor returns in dollar terms, two percentages are calculated for the period examined: total investor return rate and annualized investor return rate. Total return rate is determined by calculating the investor return dollars as a percentage of the net of the sales, redemptions and exchanges for each period.

KEY CONCEPTS OF INVESTMENT SUCCESS

The good news is that for every challenge there exists a solution—a path to navigate the potholes. While we never advocate a one-size-fits-all approach for entrepreneurs, the basic, most powerful principles are true for everyone. Depending on your specific goals, values and objectives, strategies and solutions can be developed in sync with your unique situation.

Next we'll examine in some detail the key concepts of investment success.

1. Asset allocation decisions drive long-term success

"Ninety-seven percent of performance variation is due to asset class structure." —Eugene Fama, economist and Nobel laureate in economics

The first thing you must understand as an investor who is looking to make smart financial decisions is this: The broad asset classes you choose to own (such as stocks, bonds, alternatives, real estate, private equity and so on) and the percentage of your household wealth that you allocate to each of those asset classes will have a greater impact on your future investment returns than *any* other decision you make—including which individual stocks you buy.

This means your first question as an intelligent investor must be: How should I allocate my assets among the major asset categories?

This is the single most important investment decision to be made. If it is done correctly, you should know the approximate return to expect from a given portfolio over the long run, and what a 2008-style scenario would look like in terms of drawdown and the amount of time needed to get back to even. It is this knowledge that enables you to accomplish the crucial task of tuning out the noise and remaining consistent in your approach.

Vanguard's John Bogle famously said, "Buy right and hold tight. Once you set your asset allocation, stick to it no matter how greedy or scared you become."

> Your first question as an intelligent investor must be: How should I allocate my assets among the major asset categories?

Indeed, clients sometimes ask us, "What is your plan?" for dealing with the latest troubling headlines or a downturn in the stock market. Our answer is always the same: The plan—driven by our investment philosophy statement (ours is about 42 pages long)—was established up front when we determined the appropriate asset allocation for you and your family.

> Buy right and hold tight. Once you set your asset allocation, stick to it no matter how greedy or scared you become.
>
> John Bogle

"The most important thing about an investment philosophy is that you have one you can stick with." —David Booth, founder, Dimensional Fund Advisors

Think of your household as a new business. Your "main office" is now your family office.

> The most important thing about an investment philosophy is that you have one you can stick with.
>
> David Booth

Therefore, it makes sense to examine how other successful families tend to manage their wealth. One broad survey of single-family offices reveals that high-net-worth families allocate their investable assets as shown in the table below. This data can be a good **starting point** from which to make your own family office asset allocation decisions. Again, no two families have exactly the same needs and goals.

	Target Allocation
Stocks	44%
Bonds	15%
Hedge funds	14%
Private equity	9%
Real estate	9%
Other tangible assets	4%
Principal company investments	4%
Other stores of value	1%

Data from the Wharton Global Family Alliance

Note that the allocation to stocks for the typical family office remains relatively high, at 44 percent. We believe that this allocation to equities may be unnecessarily risky for many successful families, who might very well be able to achieve the full range of their financial goals and preserve their wealth better by owning fewer equities (for example, around 30 percent).

Take this example of an entrepreneur—we'll call him Dan—who had recently experienced a liquidity event and sold his firm. The deal was largely equity in the acquiring company—leaving him not only with a large allocation to stocks, but also with a concentrated position in a single holding. We began working toward an overall portfolio allocation that resembled the typical family office allocation, customized to his family's unique needs and goals. As homes and other assets were acquired, Dan was able to use the targeted household allocation to stay on track over a planned number of years.

2. Asset class returns are ample for preserving and growing wealth

If our asset allocation choices are responsible for nearly all of our investment results, then clearly it makes sense to build portfolios consisting of entire asset classes—be they stocks, bonds or other categories.

This was exactly the thinking that turned Wall Street upside down when John Bogle founded Vanguard. As he once said, "Don't look for the needle in the haystack. Just buy the haystack."

My experience is that people like stocks. They like the stories attached to products and companies and growth. As a result, the act of stock picking receives a tremendous amount of focus from investors and their advisors.

However, when you purchase the stock of one or even several companies, you essentially place a bet that has two possible outcomes: lose a lot or make a lot. But when you buy "the whole market"—that is,

> Don't look for the needle in the haystack. Just buy the haystack.
>
> John Bogle

the hundreds of stocks that make up a particular asset class—you vastly narrow the range of possible outcomes. It may not provide the same adrenaline rush as holding a single hot individual stock, but it certainly protects your downside while still providing plenty of upside.

Further, it is incredibly difficult to consistently pick only the winners over time. Consider these findings from the SPIVA® U.S. Scorecard:

- **84.2 percent** of large-cap stock fund managers underperformed their benchmark (the S&P 500, aka the "haystack") during the five years through 2015.

- **82.1 percent** failed to deliver incremental returns over the benchmark over the past 10 years.

- **90.1 percent** of small-cap stock fund managers lagged their benchmark (S&P SmallCap 600) during the past five years.

- **88.4 percent** underperformed over the 10-year period.

What's more, the few active stock pickers who **do** manage to beat their benchmarks in a given year are more likely to have been lucky than skillful. According to research by Nobel laureate Eugene Fama and his frequent co-author Ken French:

"An investor doesn't have a prayer of picking a manager that can deliver alpha. Even over a 20-year period, the past performance of an actively managed fund has a ton of random noise that makes it difficult, if not impossible, to distinguish luck from skill."

Add in the drag on returns from trading costs, tax inefficiency and fees paid to managers to do the stock picking, and it's no wonder that active stock pickers lag the indices that represent various asset classes. Professional money managers or otherwise, the odds of consistently outperforming the broader market are extraordinarily slim.

Is there a better way? We believe so. Suppose the market consists of thousands of different marbles—each a different color, and each with a different value that can grow or diminish. The active manager has a choice: to choose 20 or so marbles of different colors that seem to look best, or to fill the jar of marbles with many different types—i.e., to diversify.

> Even over a 20-year period, the past performance of an actively managed fund has a ton of random noise that makes it difficult, if not impossible, to distinguish luck from skill.
>
> Eugene Fama

We embrace the approach that starts with the full jar and then weeds out the undesirable ones. This is based on decades of academic research that teaches us there are different dimensions of risk that lead to different dimensions of expected returns. The focus is not on which select stocks to own, but rather on which stocks **not to own**. Added bonus? The active manager who starts with the empty jar typically also comes with high fees and a higher tax bill. Diversifying can help you avoid both of those potholes.

For the average retail investor, a Vanguard or classic index fund is optimal. Even when I was trading full time, I kept my retirement and my father's retirement account invested in index funds. Think of the more evolved version described above as an institutional (as opposed to retail) solution. Having developed a partnership with Dimensional Fund Advisors (DFA), we are now able to offer our clients the same investment sources that pension funds and endowments have utilized for decades. We believe this to be the best institutional solution for our clients. As fiduciaries, we are required to act first in our clients' best interest—not our own. That means we are not allowed to receive commissions, kickbacks or other incentives for steering our clients into DFA funds. We can't just recommend "suitable investments" for our clients—they have to be investments that are absolutely in our clients' best interests.

Dimensional only works with fiduciaries—which is why its funds aren't accessible by brokers at firms such as UBS, J.P. Morgan and Merrill Lynch. DFA has a strict vetting process for advisory firms that want to partner with it. As of this writing, we are one of only 12 firms in the Los Angeles area that DFA works with.

3. Staying invested consistently is the all-weather approach

Many of our clients reside near us in Los Angeles, where the average annual temperature is a very comfortable 65 degrees. In Southern California, our "seasons" don't vary much from the average annual temperature of 65. Other clients reside in New York City, where the average temperature is cooler, but still a very comfortable 56 degrees. However, the temperature swings are much more significant in the Big Apple, ranging from stifling heat and humidity in the summer to icy temperatures and falling snow in winter. In my home state of Indiana, a similar average of 54 degrees is skewed by even colder winters. We also have clients in Central Texas. On the surface, the average annual temperature of 66 degrees is about the same as it is in California. But in Texas, there are fiery, sticky summers and freezing, rainy winters, which means Central Texans have far fewer days at their comfortable 66-degree average than do Southern Californians.

The markets are a lot like the weather in Texas or New York City. The long-term results are just fine. Stocks have delivered average annualized returns of around 10 to 12 percent since 1926—making them the best-performing asset class by far. But rarely do we have a year in which returns are in the 10-to-12-percent range. Indeed, those "average" returns rarely occur during shorter periods of time such as one year, five years or even 10 years. Instead, investment returns are "lumpy." We have above-average periods during which returns are much higher, followed by below-average periods with much lower returns. This is how we arrive at the historical average in practice.

To maximize your chance of realizing the returns that stocks potentially offer over time, you need to invest—and stay invested—for long periods of time. Otherwise, you risk being out of the market during those robust periods when returns are well above average. As DFA founder David Booth is fond of saying, "You've already paid for the risk, so it might be good to stick around for the expected return."

Further complicating matters is the putative impossibility of predicting consistently when market surges and swoons will occur. It turns out that stock market gains are highly concentrated—a relatively small number of days are responsible for the bulk of the stock market's impressive long-term returns. Miss just a few of those key days, and your long-term returns plummet.

Say, for example, that you invested $1,000 in January 1970 in a fund that earned the same return as the S&P 500. By 2015, that $1,000 would have grown to more than $89,678, provided you left your money in that fund for the duration (see the table below). But if you had tried to time the market and were not invested during the best 25 days of each year

> You've already paid for the risk, so it might be good to stick around for the expected return.
>
> David Booth

during that period, your $1,000 would have grown to just $21,224, less than one-fourth of what you would have earned had you remained fully invested.

	Growth of $1 Invested January 1970 Through December 2015
S&P 500	$89,678
S&P 500 without best 25 days of each year	$21,224

Source: The S&P data are provided by Standard & Poor's Index Services Group.

So why is it so difficult for many to stay invested and to capture the full returns that the market offers? The fact is, humans tend to make investment decisions based on their emotions. We can blame this behavior on generations of successful marketing by financial services providers combined with human wiring.

The results, however, are decidedly bad. Consider these returns for the 20-year period through 2015:

- Stocks (S&P 500): 8.2 percent
- Bonds (Barclays US Aggregate): 5.3 percent
- Portfolio consisting of 60 percent stocks/40 percent bonds: 7.2 percent
- *Average investor return: 2.1 percent*

Returns are for the period ending December 31, 2015. Average equity investor, average bond investor and average asset allocation investor performance results are calculated using data supplied by the Investment Company Institute. Investor returns are represented by the change in total mutual fund assets after excluding sales, redemptions and exchanges. This method of calculation captures realized and unrealized capital gains, dividends, interest, trading costs, sales charges, fees, expenses and any other costs. After calculating investor returns in dollar terms, two percentages are calculated for the period examined: total investor return rate and annualized investor return rate. Total return rate is determined by calculating the investor return dollars as a percentage of the net of the sales, redemptions and exchanges for each period.

The typical investor earned far less than the underlying investments he or she owned during that 20-year period, due to actions such as poor investment selection and failed attempts to jump in and out of the financial markets at "just the right times." As Warren Buffett said, "Risk comes from not knowing what you're doing."

4. Diversification provides a smoother investment journey—and greater wealth

As noted earlier, Andrew Carnegie's advice for growing assets—put all your eggs in one basket and watch the basket—is sage wisdom when it comes to building a great enterprise. That strategy has worked for you as an entrepreneur, and it's likely why you are reading this book.

Successful investing is an entirely different story, however—one in which diversification is the key to growing (and more important, keeping) your money.

Contrary to Andrew Carnegie's advice, we all know the basic, almost cliché idea behind diversification: ***Don't*** put all your eggs in one basket.

And yet, too many investors—especially entrepreneurs—invest too much of their wealth in any number of non-diversified ways. Some of the most common, and potentially wealth-threatening, include:

1. Owning too much of any **one single stock (*i.e., overly concentrated*)**.

Dealing with concentrated stock

So-called concentrated stock positions are particularly common among business owners after they've had a liquidity event. That's often when they have received a large amount of stock of the company (or companies) that acquired their enterprise. In such situations, there are two main tasks for the successful entrepreneur:

1. Reducing your overall portfolio's allocation to stocks.

2. Reducing your single-stock exposure and the company-specific risk that accompanies it.

A plan should be developed to diversify into other asset classes as well as into other categories of equities.

Often, the best approach for dealing with an oversized position in one stock is one or a combination of the following strategies:

1. **Fixed selling program.** This commonly used approach involves the scheduled selling of fixed amounts of stock at regular intervals, and can be customized by time and quantity.

2. **Custom scale-out strategy.** This involves capping a concentrated stock position at a fixed percentage of household wealth, and selling a portion of the position to trim it back as higher prices are achieved. With this approach, you will always maintain a core position in the stock—a potential benefit if the stock posts strong multiyear gains.

3. **Using options** to protect downside or realized upside at certain price targets. Options can be bought individually (i.e., a protective put or hedge against a drop in the price of a certain security), or can be used in combination (i.e., "collaring"). Although the complexities and tax implications increase with this strategy, options are an excellent way to assist a selling program.

4. **Using algorithms.** Market timing risk can be reduced, and market impact minimized, when selling large blocks of stock by using algorithmic programs. Simply put, an average price over a specified period (a full trading day) can be targeted, monitored through the day and realized as a single trade.

2. Owning too much of any **one single asset class**, such as stocks or alternatives.

3. Owning **too many stocks from one single industry**, sector or country.

In all the above scenarios, the investors are taking on far more risk than is prudent. It is simply unnecessary to incur the full volatility of a single asset class, like stocks. The marginal benefit from doing so (in the form of higher return) is not commensurate with the amount of risk taken—risk that can threaten the preservation of your wealth.

No one can say what will happen today, tomorrow or next month with absolute certainty. Unexpected developments will always occur that can affect your investments in ways you might never anticipate.

Therefore, it's impossible to know precisely when a stock, asset class or industry will outrun all the others—and when it will find itself languishing at the back of the pack. In fact, financial science tells us that an asset class that soars in one year rarely finds itself at the top of the pack the following year. Likewise, a "loser" asset class one year often catapults to the winner's circle the next year.

The lesson that financial science teaches us is clear: If you want to own winning investments consistently over time, you can't just invest in one or two stocks, sectors or even broad asset classes. You need to own many of them at all times—regardless of how they perform in any single year.

That way, you will always be invested in enough areas of the market that are doing relatively well at any given moment.

Diversifying your portfolio will also ensure that you don't put too much of your money in the wrong areas of the market and end up watching your net worth plummet. With diversification, your portfolio is far less likely to experience wild swings in value the way a highly focused or highly concentrated portfolio does.

5. Global exposure adds value

During the so-called "lost decade" of 2000-2009, the S&P 500 delivered a cumulative total return of *minus* 9.1 percent. Add in the volatility of two sizable bear markets during that time, and nobody remembers that period too fondly.

Interestingly, however, other asset classes fared much better than large-cap U.S. stocks over the same dark period:

MSCI World ex-US Index   + 17.5 percent

MSCI Emerging Markets Index   + 154.3 percent

Citigroup World Gov't Bond Index + 57.7 percent

A properly balanced portfolio diversified across the globe and asset classes had a much better chance of not losing an entire decade. Looking outside the United States can feel uncertain and be intimidating for many. Headlines can be frightening, and foreign governments unpredictable. In an agnostic investment portfolio, however, it is exactly in these environments that value is found. If one doesn't make the mistake of having too many opinions and diversifying improperly, history shows, a global portfolio will tend to weather any storm quite well. We have the ability to own 12,000 stocks in 44 countries through a select number of low-cost institutional asset class funds for our clients. The bond market exposure via these funds is equally broad. This way you can feel like the house, rather than an individual gambler. When you participate in all markets, the odds are more likely to be in your favor. You don't need to decide when to walk away from the ace or the jack or when to turn off the "let the gamblers gamble." Over the long term, the house always wins.

6. Diversify with fixed income

"Rule No. 1: Never lose money. Rule No. 2: Never forget rule No. 1."
—Warren Buffett

There are many definitions of risk. Too many, actually. We concern ourselves with two types:

1) Fluctuations in the value of a portfolio

2) Actual realized losses in a portfolio

The latter type of risk results from owning single stocks of companies that experience major financial issues (like Bear Stearns, Lehman Brothers, Countrywide, Enron, eToys, etc.) and has no place in our process. The former can be tolerated differently by different investors, and is the type of risk we can do something about.

> Rule #1: Never lose money.
>
> Rule #2: Never forget rule #1.
>
> Warren Buffett

For this type of risk, we allocate to bonds. That's because bond prices typically do not fluctuate as much as do stock prices, and they often rise when stocks fall—making bonds excellent tools for diversification and for smoothing out overall portfolio returns. In the 2007-2008 bear market, for example, stocks lost more than 50 percent of their value. In sharp contrast, the Barclays US Aggregate Bond Index delivered a 6.1 percent annualized return during that time, while the highest-quality long-term U.S. government bonds returned 17.6 percent per year.

Overall, bonds historically generate lower returns than do stocks over the long term. And with interest rates near historic lows right now, you may wonder how bonds could do anything but hurt the overall return of your portfolio going forward. But that question doesn't account for the uncertainty of *time*. The long-term return expectations for stocks and bonds are not valid for each and every starting point in history. Plus, we never know how far—or for how long—any asset class will trend up or down. Remember from above that investment returns are "lumpy" and unpredictable? It's entirely possible that even a low annual return from bonds of, say, 3 percent over the next few years could end up giving your portfolio a boost and help you better preserve wealth if stocks experience multiple years of flat or negative returns.

That's exactly what happened during the decade-long period from 1965 through 1975. During that time, U.S. government bonds returned 2.2 percent annually. Hardly impressive—but still better than the 1.2 percent annualized return from stocks over the period. Ancient history? Maybe. But there's no way to be sure history won't repeat.

The message: By owning bonds at all times—even when they appear unattractive—you could at any time own the best-performing asset class available, and therefore preserve your wealth better while increasing the probability of generating the target return you seek from your portfolio.

7. Control what you can control

You may not be able to control the direction of the market, but (as shown throughout this chapter) you can control the level of risk that you bear and how you position your wealth to best take advantage of the market to compensate you for that risk. Other key determinants of your investment success that you can—and should—seek to control include:

- **Costs.** Focus on the total cost structure of your investments with the goal of minimizing all components as much as possible—such as portfolio expense ratios, trading costs, fund turnover and tax-related costs. Asset class funds that maintain consistent exposure to various segments of the financial markets have cost-advantageous features such as low expenses and low turnover that enable more of your investment capital to be put to work.

- **Taxes.** Tax efficiency offers a tremendous opportunity to add value by minimizing drag on a portfolio. One way to boost overall tax efficiency is to use tax-sensitive and tax-optimized investments that keep trades to a minimum and keep taxable gains low through advanced trading strategies. Because you are likely in a high tax bracket, this focus on after-tax returns becomes especially important. To that end, municipal bonds might be more heavily weighted within the fixed-income portion of the portfolio, while "yield plays" such as bank loans and high-yield corporate debt may be de-emphasized.

There are some one-size-fits-all "tax efficiency" models that rarely serve entrepreneurs well. Instead, entrepreneurs require specialized customization to their unique situation, which is often complex with a lot of moving parts. We have an arsenal of tools that help to minimize taxes, but many require customization to the individual or family.

COORDINATE AND OVERSEE— THE PERSONAL CFO

Many affluent families work with multiple financial advisors and/or money managers. For example, 78 percent of families with more than $10 million in investable assets have more than three advisors simultaneously, according to CEG Worldwide. This "advisor diversification" approach may make good sense in some situations.

That said, the key to working with multiple financial professionals simultaneously is to ensure that all of your professionals' efforts are coordinated. That way, an investment strategy implemented by one advisor doesn't conflict with or harm an investment solution used by another. As noted in Chapter 2, a personal CFO is needed here—someone who is capable of organizing, overseeing and coordinating the work that all of your professionals do on behalf of you and your family. The real value in your investment experience comes from this coordination, which helps ensure that every investment strategy works as it should and nothing falls between the cracks. Without a trusted personal CFO at the top, the good work of all the other professionals can be quickly negated.

THE NEXT STEPS

As you know from Chapter 2, the Investment Consulting process is just the first step in a Collaborative Wealth Management Process. Once your investment foundation is built and solidified, it's time to turn your attention to the key *non-investment* financial areas of importance in your life.

These areas might include enhancing wealth through savvy tax planning, transferring wealth to family members or others, protecting wealth from those who would seek to take it from you, and donating wealth to causes and organizations you care about.

The next chapter will focus on these key advanced planning issues. It will show you how the Collaborative Wealth Management Process enables you to coordinate your decisions in these areas with your overall investment plan to achieve maximum benefits.

C h a p t e r

4

ADVANCED PLANNING: ADDRESSING YOUR OTHER KEY FINANCIAL CHALLENGES

K e y   T a k e a w a y s :

■ To be financially successful, entrepreneurs should heed five major non-investment concerns: tax mitigation, wealth transfer, wealth protection, succession planning and charitable giving.

■ Strategies to address these concerns run the gamut—including trusts, tax wrappers, umbrella policies, LLCs and many others.

■ The strategies used to address each of these issues must be coordinated so one solution doesn't negate or erode the effectiveness of another.

By now, you've seen how hugely important the ideal investment plan can be to helping you meet your goals. The right investment strategies set you up to preserve your money.

But when it comes to your long-term financial health and well-being, investments are only part of the picture. To make sure every part of your financial life is firing on all cylinders and working in a smooth, coordinated manner, you need to go beyond just the world of stocks, bonds and even complex alternative investments.

Remember that true Collaborative Wealth Management encompasses three key components:

1. Investment Consulting
2. Advanced Planning
3. Relationship Management

In this chapter, we'll explore the second of those components—**Advanced Planning**. This component of the Collaborative Wealth Management Process addresses the broad range of financial needs that you have *beyond* your investment portfolio.

Advanced Planning is one of the most satisfying things for us to help clients with. It's where we can make the biggest impact for our clients, for their families and sometimes for the world at large.

A well-crafted advanced plan adds real value to your life not only by addressing your crucial non-investment issues, but also by coordinating them so that each piece of your financial life works with all the others seamlessly. That way, for example, your investment portfolio's structure will reflect your estate planning goals or your plans for your business during the coming year.

The end result: All parts of your financial life work in concert to provide you with the maximum positive impact that you need to achieve your goals and to enjoy peace of mind.

FIVE ADVANCED AREAS OF CONCERN

Empirical research, combined with my own experience helping successful entrepreneurs and their families manage their wealth, has brought me to this important conclusion: There are five broad categories of non-investment issues that most successful entrepreneurs need to prioritize.

1. Tax mitigation
2. Wealth transfer
3. Wealth protection
4. Succession planning
5. Charitable giving

Through our Mutual Discovery Process, we identify where you are today and where you want to be in the future. Our role is to help you bridge the gaps in each of the five areas above to get you where you want to go.

1. Tax mitigation. You don't just need to make money. You also need to keep, save and invest it. So it's no surprise that minimizing the amount of taxes you pay is a big concern for successful entrepreneurs. Yet research shows that **more than five out of six entrepreneurs (85 percent) do not do any tax planning in advance of a liquidity event**. Mitigating income, estate and capital gains taxes is a focal point for accomplished entrepreneurs and their families.

> You don't just need to make money. You also need to keep, save and invest it.

2. Wealth transfer. Many accomplished entrepreneurs are looking beyond their own financial needs. They want to ensure that their heirs, parents, children and grandchildren are well taken care of with minimal difficulty and cost, and in accordance with their wishes. According to Vanguard, more than half of affluent Americans say that their kids' and grandkids' financial situations are a concern.[4] And yet, **too many successful entrepreneurs have no formal estate or giving plans**. If they do, those plans are often outdated and don't reflect current conditions and needs. Remember, estate planning is not a one-time event; it's something you must review every three to five years. It's not necessarily enjoyable, but remember that your life never stops changing.

3. Wealth protection. No matter where you're from or how you made your wealth, you can be a target for a host of unscrupulous people. Many affluent investors, including entrepreneurs, are worried about keeping their assets safe from potential creditors, litigants, children's spouses, ex-spouses, and disgruntled former employees and partners, as well as from catastrophic losses that could cripple them financially.

4. Succession planning. Only 30 percent of family-held and closely held businesses survive into the second generation. Just 12 percent are still viable into the third generation, and a mere 3 percent operate into the fourth generation or beyond.[5] Those statistics are even more disturbing because the same research shows that the vast majority of business families are overly optimistic—they believe they *will* be in control of their companies five years hence. Given this gloomy success record for family business transitions, it is no wonder that 60 to 70 percent of family wealth is lost by the second generation and that 90 percent is lost by the third generation.[6] It does not have to be this way.

As I have discussed elsewhere in this book, the time to start thinking about what's next for you is well before the time you plan to exit your business. Your wealth advisor, or even a financial therapist, can help you start thinking about the next chapter in your life—well before it's time to turn to that page. Do you want to start a foundation? Do you want to launch another venture? Do you want to advise companies or serve on boards? It's essential that you keep learning and have a clear purpose throughout your life.

5. Charitable giving. A growing number of successful people like you want to have a major positive impact in their communities and on the world at large. Facilitating and increasing the effectiveness of charitable intent is very important to a burgeoning segment of high-net-worth investors. Research shows that charitable giving rose for the fifth consecutive year to a record $373 billion in 2016.

CRAFTING AN ADVANCED PLAN

Given the broad areas of concern that most entrepreneurs face, a properly designed advanced plan will spell out various steps to take to address your full range of financial concerns in the following five areas:

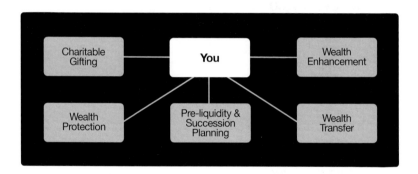

1. Wealth enhancement. This is the process of lowering your tax bill by using strategies to maximize the tax efficiency of your current assets and cash flow, taking into account your growth and wealth preservation needs. Some of the most common objectives of wealth enhancement include maximizing your assets to realize financial goals and minimizing the exposure of your assets to unnecessary taxes.

The ultimate goal of wealth enhancement, of course, is to keep more of your money in your own pocket, and to give less to the government.

Accomplishing these goals can involve any number of approaches. You (or you and the team of professionals you work with) might review your past tax returns and perform a current-year tax assessment to develop scenario planning for various strategies that you may be contemplating as you go through life. You might examine the effectiveness of your cash management procedures, or analyze an executive compensation program or a benefits plan to ensure that you are maximizing any investments and tax-advantaged vehicles.

Many of our clients have gone through this process with us, and we take a few simple steps to help lessen what Uncle Sam receives and maximize what our clients keep in their bank and brokerage accounts.

Let's use the hypothetical example of Fred and Frieda, a couple that acquired a sizable portfolio that they won't need to tap for several years. Unfortunately, the portfolio was being eroded by federal, state and local taxes, so we created a "tax wrapper" that allowed the portfolio's assets to grow tax-deferred. In the future, this money could be accessed tax-free by way of a loan. With proper planning, the appreciation can avoid gift and estate tax.

In the past, tax wrappers and other sophisticated

strategies would have been available only to the Super Rich (individuals and families whose net worth exceeds $500 million). Thanks to technology and scale, many of these advanced tax mitigation strategies can be utilized by entrepreneurs who have a significant net income or liquidity event. This is especially helpful, as these entrepreneurs tend to be in the highest tax bracket.

This result may not be appropriate for you, of course. It depends on your own unique situation. The key is not to take anything for granted and to assemble a knowledgeable team of experts that can work on your behalf—and work well together.

2. Wealth transfer. This area is focused on ways to structure your assets effectively for their eventual transfer to others. It's also where you facilitate the most tax-efficient ways to pass assets—including business assets, company stock and other owners' equity—to succeeding generations in your family, and to other people and causes that you care about, in a way that satisfies your wishes and desires.

The current top federal estate tax rate is 40 percent. Beyond a certain dollar amount, this rate can apply to everything on your personal balance sheet. That includes assets you may not have even considered, such as artwork, privately held businesses that you built from scratch and the vacation home that you and your family enjoy.

To address wealth transfer issues, you need to answer important questions that you may not have considered (or that you would prefer to ignore). Examples: How do you want your assets to be distributed when you are no longer here? How and when should your heirs receive an inheritance? How can your liquidity needs be met if your estate is illiquid? If you have a privately held company, how will your family pay the tax bill? Maybe you've acquired a substantial art collection. Could the current value be exposed to estate tax and trigger an unwanted liquidation?

Action steps here can include:

- Determining your wealth transfer preferences.

- Identifying any special situations you may face (such as a special-needs child).

- Examining your business succession issues.

- Considering a range of trusts, insurance policies or partnerships that ensure effective transfer.

Strategies you can use to achieve wealth transfer goals range from basic estate planning (such as credit-shelter trusts and traditional life insurance) to more sophisticated techniques (such as self-canceling installment notes, remainder purchase marital trusts, and generation-skipping trusts with life insurance).

Consider, for example, the topic of wills and trusts. A will is a legal document that clearly explains how a person wants his or her estate to distribute assets after death. By contrast, a trust is a pool of assets (it might be investments, cash, property, etc.) that are held for the benefit of a third party—the beneficiary. A trustee is appointed to oversee the management of the trust. If you create the trust during your lifetime, then it is known as a "living trust" and initially you are the one who fulfills the roles of both trustee and beneficiary. When creating the trust, you establish how you want the trust to distribute your assets after you die.

While wills and trusts can accomplish similar estate planning objectives, **a trust is generally more flexible than a will** and allows you to exert greater control over the distribution of your assets. Suppose you want to leave a large sum of money to your son, daughter or close relative who is a minor. Unlike a will, a trust can establish how and when the child will receive the money after you're gone. You can also set up a trust to fulfill specific objectives, such as paying for a child's education. A properly structured trust can also help your heirs avoid certain estate taxes and stay out of probate court. That said, trusts generally cost more than wills to set up and are usually more complex. It's also important to follow through on funding a trust and re-titling assets owned by the trust. If you don't, many of the potential benefits of a trust won't be realized.

There are a variety of trusts you can set up. While having a living trust can be great, it's possible that you may need to continue with some further advanced planning that is more sophisticated.

Let's look at Bill and Barb, who built a great business together from scratch. When we asked Bill and Barb who was important to them, they immediately mentioned their children—we'll call them Amy and Andy. When we probed the couple for details, they said they didn't want to spoil their children by giving them a windfall of cash. At the same time, they wanted to ensure that their kids would never to have to worry about money. As Warren Buffett loves to say: ***"Give children enough to do anything, but not enough to do nothing."***

Bill and Barb told us that their daughter Amy, a social worker, and son Andy, an artist, have been financially responsible and self-supporting. They didn't foresee any issues with the kids, but they admitted they were slightly concerned about the influence that some of their children's wealthy friends might have on them—young people who "treat an inheritance like a lottery ticket," they lamented.

> Give children enough to do anything, but not enough to do nothing.
>
> Warren Buffett

This was uncharted territory for Bill and Barb. On the tax side, we immediately identified a big problem: Their

$50 million family business could trigger a $15 million tax bill without proper planning. As a solution, we looked to transfer interest in the business to the children via a trust—which is very flexible. Bill and Barb continued to maintain full control of the business and the income it generated. The tax code (as of the writing of this book) still allows you to transfer most of your business interests to your kids on a discounted basis, thereby allowing you to get much more of your money to your children and shield more of it from the government. This allowed Bill and Barb to reduce by millions of dollars the estate taxes that the kids would have to pay in the future.

The other challenge in Bill and Barb's situation was the children and their values. The flexibility in the trust allowed for all types of governors and restrictions to be put in place to protect Amy and Andy from things like divorce and irresponsible large money decisions, while at the same time incentivizing them to pursue their art and their charitable causes. This strategy gave Bill and Barb time to contemplate and discuss their concerns further. We also introduced them to a financial therapist with experience in this area who is part of our firm's expert network.

Please note that as we go to print, there is legislation on the table to change the rules about how business assets are transferred to children, and it may not be good for the affluent. Bottom line: The window of opportunity may be closing if you're considering a privately held business transfer. The key here is to take action and assemble a coordinated team of experts if you haven't done so already.

There is still more you can do. Sam Walton founded WalMart. The current net worth of Walton's heirs is nearly $150 billion, according to *Forbes*. Through proper planning, Walton's family managed to avoid tens of billions of dollars in estate taxes. One component of this strategy was Walton's use of trusts, such as the "Jackie O" trust strategy (named for Jacqueline Kennedy Onassis), which is charitable in nature and can help to minimize gift and estate taxes—or eliminate them entirely in some cases. Several well-known families, including an NFL team owner I know, a hedge fund manager and others, have used "Jackie O" trusts to protect their assets from estate taxes.

Notice how all of these areas work together. For example, strategies to maximize your charitable intent can sometimes be coordinated with estate planning strategies that are designed to maximize the amount of money you can give to your children down the road. This makes good sense. After all, the various parts of your financial life don't operate in a vacuum—so you shouldn't plan on managing them on your own.

3. Wealth protection. This area involves strategies you can use to ensure that your wealth is not unjustly taken from you by potential creditors, litigants, ex-spouses and children's spouses. This component of advanced planning is also designed to protect your wealth against catastrophic loss. Identity theft is another emerging threat to wealth protection that should be addressed.

Common actions you might take to protect your wealth include controlling risks though business processes, employment agreements and buy-sell agreements. You can also restructure various assets and consider legal forms of ownership—such as trusts, limited liability entities and more—that can put your wealth beyond the reach of creditors and others who might pursue it.

Insurance can also offer you protection, of course. In addition to key man/key person insurance for your business, your business and family might need (or require you to have) additional insurance for high-risk adrenaline-pumping hobbies such as auto-racing, surfing, hang gliding, back-country skiing and powerboat racing. Property and casualty (P&C) insurance can cover everything from the obvious (autos, homes) to the exotic (expensive artwork, high-end yachts). Even something as simple as rental properties should be protected by P&C insurance. If a renter's dog bites a neighbor, for example, you could be liable if your insurance coverage is simply a typical homeowners policy. However, by setting up a special umbrella policy, you could avoid liability and protect your assets more completely.

When it comes to umbrella policies, even affluent, successful people are under the impression that such policies are very expensive. You'd be surprised how much valuable protection they provide policy holders. Many successful entrepreneurs I know have umbrella policies with only $1 million to $2 million in coverage. That's really not enough, considering their current—or soon to be received—wealth. It only costs slightly more to get a $3 million, $5 million or $10 million umbrella policy. Insurers are now providing umbrellas with coverage as high as $100 million for their most affluent and successful clients.

Think of an umbrella policy as a litigation insurance policy. Unfortunately, accidents happen all the time. After speaking with a number of personal injury attorneys about how their businesses work, I've learned that they typically look at the potential payout from an umbrella policy as the "easy money." Therefore, if the umbrella is large enough, then the personal injury lawyers will go for that covered amount. That's why matching your umbrella policy to your net worth can be a wise move. Again, if cost has been holding you back from investing in an umbrella policy, know that they're surprisingly affordable, and they provide you with tremendous bang for the buck.

To help make your umbrella policy more affordable, consider raising the deductibles on your other lines of insurance—such as P&C and auto. Increasing your deductibles on other policies is a form of self-insurance with a ***defined amount of risk***. However, self-insuring by not having sufficient umbrella coverage opens you up to an **unlimited amount of risk**.

Other asset protection strategies include the creation of trusts in "trust-friendly" states such as Delaware to shield

Avoiding a "Madoff" situation

Many of you are currently (or soon will be) coming into a once-in-a-lifetime liquidity windfall. It's a huge reward for your vision and hard work. So protecting your wealth becomes even more important.

Here are some essential questions to ask yourself, your controller and your financial advisor:

a.) Do you have custody of my assets?

b.) Who's your third-party custodian?

c.) Does this custodian provide statements independent of your advisor's firm?

d.) Will any of the investments that you make result in another advisor having custody of my assets? Sometimes advisors place money with other advisors, who may then have custody. Unfortunately, this is how a lot of people unknowingly get into trouble. Asking the question up front can head off negative surprises later.

Sad to say, you'll likely be offered at least one "investment opportunity of a lifetime" in the next 12 months that lacks appropriate controls. Unless there is a Big Four accounting firm auditing the numbers and financial statements of the controlling entity, I strongly recommend letting this "once-in-a-lifetime opportunity" pass. Caveat emptor!

From Anthony Glomski article in Nasdaq.com

assets from creditors. This advanced planning technique is sophisticated, but it can add a nearly bulletproof layer of protection to your assets and tends to be underutilized by well-off people with potentially a lot to lose.

4. Pre-liquidity and succession planning. This is typically where we see the biggest gap and the most lost opportunity. According to AES Nation (Accelerating Entrepreneurial Success), more than five out of six entrepreneurs (85 percent) fail to do sufficient tax planning prior to the sale of their businesses. While you probably have a CPA and an estate attorney, chances are you don't have someone to coordinate the work of your CPA, estate attorney and other financial experts—less than 15 percent of successful entrepreneurs do, according to AES.

Unless business succession planning is approached in a coordinated way, your wealth can be eroded significantly by income, capital gains, IRD (income in respect of a decedent), gift, estate and other taxes. In many privately held successful businesses, the company will generate taxable cash flow to the owners that exceeds what is needed to fund the owner's lifestyle. This extra cash flow can be taxed at 50 percent or higher (top marginal state and federal income tax rates). When the after-tax proceeds are invested, the growth is subject to capital gains rates of 30 percent or higher after taking into account state tax rates, the Medicare surtax and the phase-out of deductions. Ultimately, when the remaining assets are passed to family members or successor managers, there could be a 40 percent gift or estate tax applied.

To help solve this wealth-eroding problem, **every entrepreneur should establish a clear vision for his or her transition and look for ways to minimize the taxes**. Tax-efficient planning strategies are needed to guide decisions about daily operations and business exit strategies. An astute advisor knows how to fund business succession agreements in ways that can generate current income tax deductions while allowing the business to generate tax-free income for the business owner and/or successors.

There's also the emotional side of selling a business. Many conflicts can erode family and business relationships, especially when a founder (or founders) is preparing to step away from day-to-day operations. If the founder's children or siblings are highly involved in the company, succession is more often "assumed" than prepared for. The same goes for a very early employee who has been working faithfully at your company since day one. He or she may have risen patiently through the ranks and sacrificed a great deal of nights, weekends and salary to make your company a success. But suppose you don't feel that person has the chops to be the next CEO or president. Imagine his or her resentment at being passed over for the corner office for an outsider or a non-family employee.

Early in my career, I had a colleague we'll call Bill. Bill's father founded a greeting card business. Through years of hard work, Bill's dad built a company that was generating several million in sales each year. Sadly, Bill's father passed away unexpectedly and never put a true succession plan in place. It was more of a handoff to Bill and his three siblings without clear direction about who was responsible for what.

Bill, being a savvy financial professional, decided to shop the company for sale. He received an offer of $10 million, but was overruled by a sibling who insisted that the family should continue running the business. Within 18 months, the once-successful greeting card enterprise failed and the $10 million offer made to the family two years prior had evaporated. I have seen uncoordinated business succession plans and mishandled exits create havoc in personal relationships, tear family bonds apart and destroy business possibilities. Messy exits can hurt a loving family and its thriving business. Don't let this happen to you and the company you've worked so hard to build.

5. Charitable giving is all about helping you fulfill your philanthropic goals—and maximizing the effectiveness of any charitable intent you have. The idea is to use strategies that enable you to give larger amounts than you would have been able to give otherwise. The actions involved in a charitable giving strategy include evaluating your charitable options and how they fit in with your other goals, such as retirement income needs and wealth transfer goals. Various trusts, funds, foundations and gifting methods—including private foundations, donor-advised funds, charitable remainder trusts and charitable lead trusts—are routinely used to make sure your giving has the maximum impact you want it to have.

Here is an example of utilizing effective charitable giving with tax efficiency:

Like many of our clients, Tom and Tina are very charitably inclined. In recent years, they have contributed $100,000 annually to various causes they support. As California residents, they are subject to taxes on more than 50 percent of what they earn. So their philanthropic efforts have provided them with a nice tax break along with the satisfaction of supporting worthy people and organizations.

Tom and Tina's goal was to maintain their annual giving of $100,000 a year after a liquidity event. They have a large chunk of appreciated stock in their company. By pushing the stock into a private foundation, they pay no taxes when the stock is sold. In addition, they get a write-off for the stock they contributed to the foundation, which is especially helpful for mitigating the tax bill when it coincides with a large liquidity event.

In this case, Tom and Tina accomplished many goals:

1. They were able to maintain their annual gifting at the level they desired.

2. They dramatically reduced their tax bill in a high tax year.

3. They were able to lower their overall tax rate to 30 percent from 50 percent after exiting the business, using trusts and other advanced planning techniques.

4. Accelerating the deduction provided them with immediate and accelerated tax savings.

There also are options that aren't entirely philanthropy based, but which are still designed to support causes and interests about which people are passionate.

For example, you can mimic what Facebook's Mark Zuckerberg (and eBay's Pierre Omidyar before him) did: set up a limited liability company (LLC) for charitable giving. This approach comes without the tax deductions that are part of some of the other options noted above, but it allows for maximum flexibility. Think of it as a sort of "private foundation 2.0," in which the LLC structure allows philanthropists to use their money just about any way they see fit—including as investments in for-profit companies that are trying to solve societal challenges. (In contrast, strictly charitable vehicles only allow donors to make grants to tax-exempt nonprofits.) (See article in Appendix.)

A FULLY COORDINATED FINANCIAL LIFE

A Collaborative Wealth Management plan that includes both investment strategies and non-investment strategies can be tremendously valuable for your financial life. By coordinating all the components that impact and influence your financial security, you will put yourself in the best possible position to achieve the most important goals you have set for yourself as well as for your family, your business, your community and the people and organizations you care deeply about. Just as important, you will have peace of mind knowing that you are set up to succeed.

You might also be starting to see just how complex a job it is to oversee the many areas of your financial and charitable life. There's no question that it takes significant expertise to make smart decisions about everything from investment planning to tax planning to transferring, safeguarding and donating wealth effectively.

Here again is why the role of the personal CFO, mentioned in Chapter 2, is so important to your financial health. A personal CFO should be able to help you craft a long-range wealth management plan that meets your needs and goals—and build an ongoing relationship that ensures your needs continue to be met as they change over time. A key part of that responsibility is to oversee and manage the efforts of those professionals who will implement the advanced planning strategies related to wealth enhancement, wealth transfer, wealth protection, succession planning and charitable giving.

In the next chapter, we'll explore the third component of the Collaborative Wealth Management Process—relationship management. This is the part of the process that helps you (and your wealth manager, if you work with one) coordinate a team of expert professionals who can implement all the tools and strategies you need.

COLLABORATIVE WEALTH MANAGEMENT PROCESS

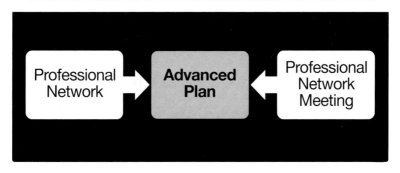

RELATIONSHIP MANAGEMENT: FINDING THE IDEAL TEAM OF EXPERTS FOR YOUR UNIQUE NEEDS

Key Takeaways:

■ Most entrepreneurs find they need four foundational members on their expert team—a wealth
manager, a private client lawyer, a CPA and an
insurance specialist.

■ A personal CFO ensures that those experts
collaborate and that their financial strategies and
recommendations work together seamlessly.

■ Look for four qualities in every member of an
expert team you work with: the right expertise, integrity/professionalism, teamwork and
compatibility.

By now, you've gained a solid understanding of the
many financial issues and challenges that you face as an

entrepreneur who is approaching a liquidity event. What's more, you have seen the process that goes into addressing those challenges in a manner that coordinates your entire financial life—from your investments all the way through your broader non-investment issues.

As you seek to implement solutions in these areas, consider all the tasks that must be accomplished in order to maximize the probability of achieving what is most important to you. Among other responsibilities, it is essential to:

- **Build, monitor and manage your household balance sheet**—including your investment portfolio and real estate and any other business interests—in a way that adequately preserves the wealth you have created and realized.

- **Design a plan for reducing the impact of taxes** as you experience a sudden and dramatic increase in your wealth, and for optimizing your tax situation post-exit—while maintaining the flexibility to address continually changing tax code rules.

- **Create a multipronged estate planning strategy** (often a series of trusts and other solutions) to ensure that your heirs and others close to you will be well taken care of and financially secure after you are gone. You also want to ensure that the government doesn't erode 40 percent of your wealth. This strategy should also be reviewed and updated to reflect new laws and regulations.

- **Construct a wealth protection plan** that effectively digs a moat around you and your wealth to guard your assets from those who might take them unjustly.

- **Craft an approach to philanthropic giving** that empowers you and your wealth to have a tremendous impact on your community, and perhaps even on the world at large.

- **Create a family wealth plan** that helps you instill wise financial values in your children and heirs as they potentially realize significant wealth. You don't want them to become stereotypical "trust fund kids."

- **Develop a life plan** post-liquidity event that ensures you continue to have meaning and purpose in your life. You don't want to feel disconnected and depressed, as some entrepreneurs do, just because you're no longer running the business you worked so hard to build and nurture.

Not exactly a trivial to-do list, is it?

The good news is you don't have to take these steps alone. In fact, trying to "fly solo" will greatly work against your best interests as a successful entrepreneur who is looking to make smart decisions about your money.

Instead, you'll want to work with the right team of professionals to implement these and other key steps in your financial life. By enlisting the help of talented professionals at the right times, you will put yourself on a path to a lifetime of financial comfort, peace of mind and meaning.

Remember that the Collaborative Wealth Management Process consists of three parts (Investment Consulting, Advanced Planning and Relationship Management) as shown in the formula below:

Wealth Management (WM) =
Investment Consulting (IC) + Advanced Planning
(AP)+ Relationship Management (RM)

Relationship Management, the focus of this chapter, is all about getting the right guidance to manage your entire financial life over the long haul. It means meeting your most important financial needs by creating and working with a team of financial experts—true professionals who have deep knowledge in the full range of issues with which you require help.

WHY DO YOU NEED A TEAM?

There are many compelling reasons to build a team of experts that can help you implement wealth management. For one, many of the tasks that you need to accomplish in order to build and maintain a strong financial future for yourself and your family are complex and time-consuming—for example, creating estate plans and implementing strategies to minimize taxes without incurring IRS scrutiny. These jobs can't be done well by you on the weekends or even by "average" professionals with a general knowledge of finance. They demand a very high level of ongoing specialized expertise and focus.

What's more, any solutions that you **do** implement need to work together with other solutions you have in place (or intend to put into motion). Otherwise, a decision you make in one area could have negative financial results in another area. This often happens when a business owner assembles a collection of professional advisors who work in their own silos, never coordinating their efforts with the others, and simply provide their advice piecemeal to the client.

These "silo" advisors usually like to work independently because it's easier for them to convince the client to use their preferred solutions without having any of the other experts weighing in or providing oversight. Some of these solutions are great, while others may be a ticking time bomb. For example, an estate plan must also involve careful tax planning. Estate attorneys—who may do an excellent job of facilitating the transfer of your money after you aren't around anymore—may not know about or be able to execute the best possible tax strategies.

Having someone to coordinate and review an integrated team's efforts is crucial. That's why our firm acts as each client's personal CFO, leading the team's efforts and coordinating the actions of the various professionals. It's not uncommon for successful entrepreneurs to work with multiple advisors. But in such cases, someone needs to take charge and provide the full financial picture to the other professionals involved in helping the client. Using a coordinated team will also minimize the likelihood of falling into "check the box" syndrome—which happens when an entrepreneur makes a decision about his or her situation and assumes it can be crossed off the list entirely. A well-coordinated team of experts knows that each one's strategies may need to be reevaluated as laws and rules change over time.

The second reason having a personal CFO is so important is that no single person—*not even the smartest advisor on the planet*—can be a true expert in all of the investment and advanced planning solutions that today's successful people and their families require. Most advisors, wealth managers, CPAs and other financial professionals won't share this fact with you, but it's true.

Think about all of the issues and strategies involved in investments, wealth enhancement, wealth protection, wealth transfer and charitable giving that were profiled in earlier chapters of this book. How realistic is it to expect a single professional to have the knowledge and skills needed to navigate all five of those areas? Sure, a world-class investment manager may know a few smart tax strategies—but chances are he or she will have little to no experience using advanced asset protection solutions

No single person—not even the smartest advisor on the planet—can be a true expert in all of the investment and advanced planning solutions that today's successful people and their families require.

that safeguard wealth after a liquidity event. Likewise, a top-flight CPA who can help you save large sums in taxes may have only a basic understanding of academic-based investment solutions that maximize your ability to preserve your wealth.

As a successful entrepreneur, you probably understand all of this intuitively. After all, you don't attempt to manage every component of your company alone. Instead, you probably hired a CFO, CTO, CMO and other key professionals to oversee the respective operational areas of your company and to give you important information, guidance and recommendations about topics on which you are **not** a deep expert.

The same dynamic should apply to your financial life. By surrounding yourself with a diverse group of specialists who have a deep understanding of their respective areas of expertise, you benefit from the best advice possible in each area. Compare that to getting help from a "jack of all trades" who is master of none.

This is true even among the very best financial advisors. Top financial advisors go out of their way to build and manage relationships with other professional experts on an ongoing basis; they don't try to do everything on their own.

In my own career as a wealth manager, I certainly don't attempt to do it all myself. Instead, I build relationships with expert professionals. Why? So I can bring the very best solutions to clients. Our clients need and want this, but often lack the time and expertise to manage an expert team of professionals effectively. If you choose to work with a financial advisor, it's crucial to select one who has the people and the resources capable of providing the advice you need.

To help make our firm uniquely suited to assisting successful entrepreneurs with their specific set of needs and concerns, we have interviewed many experts in several fields and have hand-picked those who are the best fit for our clients. We call this group our "think tank." The think tank consists of a formal panel of experts that meets regularly to brainstorm on behalf of our clients.

That said, you want to surround yourself with the right team of experts, even if you prefer to handle your finances independently and prefer not to work with a wealth manager. Even the biggest "do it yourselfers" need to find and work with specialists from time to time. We don't try to design our own website or set up our own e-commerce platform, even though we could probably figure it out eventually. Likewise, few of us have the time, training or temperament to act as our own accountants, attorneys, valuation specialists and so on.

In short, it doesn't matter who you are: It is essential for you to build relationships with professionals—and manage those relationships on an ongoing basis—if you want to achieve true, lasting and meaningful financial success for you and your family.

THE "FOUNDATIONAL FOUR" PROFESSIONALS YOU MUST HAVE ON YOUR FINANCIAL TEAM

Among entrepreneurs with complex and varied financial needs, the most successful typically work with four key professionals on a regular basis (see below). These are the experts who have the capabilities to solve the majority of the investment and advanced planning issues you are most likely to face as you pursue the next stage of your life:

1. Your wealth manager.
2. Your private client lawyer.
3. Your accountant/CPA firm—ideally, a large firm with multiple partners (preferably with a Big Four accounting background).
4. Your life insurance specialist, who is knowledgeable about current estate tax mitigation strategies.

Expert #1: Wealth manager. One of the wealth manager's most important jobs is to assemble and manage a team of expert professionals on your behalf. It's very similar to how the GM of an elite baseball team oversees the all-star players on the field. You just have to make one important choice—which wealth manager to work with—so you can tap into the collective expertise of the entire team.

For example, wealth managers who use the Collaborative Wealth Management Process described in this book focus mainly on helping investors grow and preserve their wealth through the investment consulting process. Then, to help clients meet their advanced planning needs, these wealth managers develop strong relationships with the other professionals listed below.

As the general manager of a professional network of expert resources, a wealth manager has three primary roles:

1. To select qualified professionals for the network.

2. To meet with the network of experts to develop ideal strategies for the wealth manager's clients.

3. To manage the network of experts on an ongoing basis so that these professionals are always aware of each client's current financial situation, needs and goals.

Remember: Be wary of people who tell you they can do it all themselves. Any wealth manager you work with should know enough about your situation to recognize when there may be an opportunity to add value in any or all aspects of

Remember: Be wary of people who tell you they can do it all themselves.

your financial life. However, that wealth manager should *always* have a network of experts that he or she relies on to confirm those opportunities and build strategies.

Expert #2: Private client lawyer. A private client lawyer is a hugely important member of a wealth management team. He or she is a professional who can address many of the tax, estate planning and business/legal needs of entrepreneurs experiencing (or anticipating) a liquidity event. A skilled private client lawyer will be adept at providing services like these:

- Estate planning
- Wealth protection planning
- Income tax planning
- Succession planning
- Business planning
- Developing charitable giving programs
- Probate services
- Guardianship and conservatorship services

Clearly, a lawyer who can provide these types of services can bring tremendous value to your life. Take Ben, for example, who has a special-needs child named Bobby.

Ben wants to ensure that Bobby is taken care of after Ben is gone. But Ben also has concerns because his ex-wife, Betsy, has a history of spending money on herself that was intended for Bobby's well-being. Ben worried that the funds earmarked for his son would be "accidentally" misappropriated if he weren't around to oversee them. The solution: a bulletproof trust set up to take care of Bobby indefinitely— and to prevent any financial shenanigans by Betsy or others.

Expert #3: Accountant. Unlike a private client lawyer (who will provide a big-picture perspective on tax planning), an accountant typically will have much more detailed, day-to-day knowledge of your income tax and corporate tax situation. A skilled accountant will be able to make specific recommendations to mitigate your tax exposure. This will help you pay less to the government and address some tax planning and compliance issues. Such an accountant can also recognize where to make savvy moves before and after a liquidity event. This guidance may cost you thousands of dollars, but could save you millions in the long run. The ideal accountants for successful entrepreneurs like you tend to work for large multipartner firms that have a track record of helping entrepreneurs who have gone through a variety of liquidity events. That's a different type of expertise than you find at most sole-practitioner accounting firms.

Expert #4: Life insurance specialist. A top-quality life insurance specialist will know how to identify various approaches to mitigate estate taxes and tax-deferral strategies. This specialist will often work closely with a private client lawyer to identify and structure solutions that leverage a full range of options.

For example: There's an insurance solution that acts like a "wrapper" that you can transfer assets into—thus eliminating a tax hit that could strip you of 45 percent (or more) of the gains on your wealth. In addition, this solution provides asset protection and enables you to access your assets tax-free during your lifetime. This customized wrapper allows for the inclusion of low-cost investment options (for example, Vanguard offerings) as well as other investments such as high-yield bonds, hedge funds and other investments that tend to be very tax-inefficient otherwise.

ADDITIONAL EXPERTS TO CONSIDER WHEN NEEDED

Beyond the four foundational experts (see above) who make up the core of your advisory team, there are other professionals that you will likely need to work with occasionally—or maybe just once when you are going through a liquidity event or other key transition in your life.

For example, many successful entrepreneurs find that one of the first professionals they need to add beyond the "core four" team is a **personal lines insurance specialist**—a property-casualty agent who works at the very high end of the market. In addition, you may need a **credit expert** to evaluate your current situation with one or more loans you are carrying. You might also need a **derivatives specialist** who deals with concentrated stock positions. Likewise, a **securities lawyer** may be needed to support the derivatives specialist. Sometimes an **actuary** is needed if you are dealing with certain life insurance issues. And a **valuation specialist** may be needed to appraise your business interests as you develop a succession plan.

In addition, there may be a need for an **art professional** for help with acquisition, disposition, protection, valuation and tax mitigation related to the sale and transfer of your art collection. A financial therapist may be important for helping you deal emotionally with a dramatic and sudden increase in wealth (and the insecurities it can unleash). We find that a **family governance professional** can also be vitally important in dealing with family wealth issues that impact you and your loved ones. Finally, you may want to work with a **health and wellness professional** that provides global concierge healthcare services as well as comprehensive longevity programs.

Again, these are simply examples of the types of specialists you may need post-liquidity. Depending on your unique requirements, you may need to bring in other types of experts to address highly specific challenges. That said, you don't need to have close relationships with every one of these experts or try to oversee them all. Instead, you should be able to rely on your four core team members to bring in these experts as needed.

Take a look at the chart below showing one example of the type of professional network to use in your financial life. You can see that the wealth manager is at the center, acting as the coordinator of the team and the single point of contact. His or her primary relationships are with the three other core experts: **the private client lawyer, the accountant** and the **life insurance specialist**. These team members then have relationships with the other types of specialists you may need from time to time.

A Sample Professional Network

- Charitable Giving Specialist
- Corporate Tax Lawyer

Private Client Lawyer

Wealth Manager

Accountant

Life Insurance Specialist

Other Specialists

- Actuary
- Valuation Specialist

- Personal Lines Insurance Agent
- Derivatives Specialist
- Credit Expert
- Securities Lawyer

Source: CEG Worldwide

FINDING THE RIGHT PEOPLE TO HELP

If you work with a comprehensive wealth manager, you can rely on him or her to provide you with access to a network of expert professionals to address your financial issues and needs. You could also ask your wealth manager to coordinate with other professionals with whom you currently work.

However, if you are building your own expert team from scratch, you will need to do your homework and identify good candidates in the key areas in which you need help.

Keep in mind that there are four qualities that every member of a professional network should possess: the right expertise, integrity/professionalism, teamwork and compatibility. Experts who have these four qualities will be true assets to your overall team and will be key to coordinating and integrating your entire financial life.

1. The right expertise. You need to work with experts who deeply understand the issues you face as an entrepreneur—especially the issues that surround an impending liquidity event. Don't work with a "so-so" attorney just because he or she's a friend of a friend, for example. You owe it to yourself and the people you care about to hire the highest level of expertise that you can.

2. Integrity and professionalism. Each member of the network must bring a high standard of personal and professional integrity to the table. Each specialist must handle every aspect of his or her work (within the network and with you) with a consistent and high degree of professionalism.

3. The ability to work well together. There should be good rapport between any professional you work with and the other members of your expert network. Think about it: You need your entire team to work together so that your financial life is well coordinated and all the pieces work in concert. No matter how many awards someone has won, if that person on your team isn't able play in the same sandbox as the other team members, you run the risk of having key information fall through the cracks. You increase the risk that some solutions you implement won't be coordinated with the others—potentially leaving you vulnerable. It's like having a star coder or programmer at your company with whom nobody wants to work.

4. The ability to work well with *you*. The professionals on your team should be easy to work with and respectful toward you and your family. You may get in spirited discussions with your advisors about their ideas and recommendations, and you might not take their advice every time. That's OK. But if you find yourself constantly butting heads with them, there may be a problem in terms of how much you trust and like them—and how devoted they are to helping you.

The best way to find potential specialists for your team is most likely through your entrepreneurial friends and associates—people you can trust who have been in your shoes. Of course, the experts you work with may have professional networks of their own that they can refer you to.

YOUR TEAM

By now, you can see that your financial future and the financial well-being of your family are too important to leave in the hands of a single person—regardless of how talented, smart or hardworking that person is. To give yourself the best chance of achieving all the goals that are truly important to you, you should surround yourself with an A-team of professionals that possesses the deep skills you require—a network of experts motivated to work in your best interests at every step of your journey toward financial freedom, comfort and peace of mind. You deserve nothing less.

CONCLUSION

PUTTING IT ALL TOGETHER

At the beginning of this book, I told you that you'll face new challenges, new transitions and new opportunities as you navigate your way through a liquidity event and emerge on the other side. I also emphasized that you must do everything in your power to preserve, protect and maintain the wealth that you have worked so hard to build. That way, you can use it to have a huge impact—in your life, in your family's life, in your community and even in the world at large.

You now know the framework—Collaborative Wealth Management—for making intelligent financial decisions in all areas of your wealth so that you can achieve truly meaningful life goals. It is the same framework I use with my entrepreneur clients every day to help them achieve all that is most important to them.

As you have seen, the strategies that collectively make up Collaborative Wealth Management will empower you to address your biggest financial challenges, needs and objectives—both before and after a liquidity event. When implemented through a team of high-quality experts, the Collaborative Wealth Management Process enables you to take full command of your financial future and to achieve your goals with clarity and confidence.

Again, the process pertains not only to investment management, but to addressing the advanced concerns facing successful entrepreneurs in partnership with a team of expert professionals:

> The Collaborative Wealth Management Process enables you to take full command of your financial future and to achieve your goals with clarity and confidence.

1. Minimizing income taxes on the transaction through proactive tax planning.

2. Maximizing wealth by not leaving money on the table.

3. Preserving wealth by avoiding excessive single-stock risk and other investment mistakes that can damage wealth.

4. Transferring wealth effectively and tax-efficiently to family and others you care about to ensure they are well taken care of.

5. Protecting wealth from being taken unjustly by creditors, lawsuits, children's spouses, potential ex-spouses and catastrophic loss.

YOUR NEXT STEPS

Now that you know what works when it comes to managing your wealth effectively, you have some very important decisions to make.

Think for a moment about your most important goals—the ones that, if you achieve them, will allow you to live a life that's not just financially secure but extremely meaningful and engaging. That fact that your wealth can do so much good for so many people means you owe it to yourself, your loved ones and the causes you care about to make the best possible decisions about your money, so it can have the maximum possible impact.

Armed with that insight and the information in this book, now is a good time to ask yourself the following questions:

1. Is Collaborative Wealth Management the right approach for me? What I can tell you is that in my 15 years of working with and helping entrepreneurs like you make the smartest possible financial decisions, I have found that Collaborative Wealth Management is the approach that takes the most comprehensive and far-reaching view of wealth and the decisions that must be made around it. If, like nearly every entrepreneur in the world, you have a wide range of financial needs—such as investments, tax management, estate planning, wealth protection, succession planning and charitable giving— you will likely find that Collaborative Wealth Management provides the best possible framework for helping you successfully address those areas.

This certainly has been true in my own life: Wealth management has served me well in my roles as an investor and a successful business owner seeking to create tremendous value that I can one day realize.

2. If so, what is the most effective and impactful way to implement Collaborative Wealth Management? As you probably can tell from reading this book, Collaborative Wealth Management requires a great deal of time and effort, since it includes so many components. Comprehensive plans for investments and other assets must be created. Specific solutions must be identified and implemented. And a team of experts (accountants, attorneys and other professionals who are experienced in working with entrepreneurs) must be assembled and managed to address the many complex issues that business owners and former business owners with wealth tend to face.

If you want to incorporate Collaborative Wealth Management into your financial life, you must determine the best way to do so. Certainly some people choose to manage their financial lives by themselves, and wealth management can be undertaken on a do-it-yourself basis. That said, many entrepreneurs choose to work with financial professionals who use the Collaborative Wealth Management Process in their practices.

The decision to do it yourself or to work with a professional wealth manager boils down to a few key factors:

1. *Time.* Do you have the time to implement wealth management successfully, as outlined in this book? Are you able to devote the time needed to make these things happen—or are there other

responsibilities in your life that should be given (or need to be given) a higher priority?

The decision to do it yourself or to work with a professional wealth manager boils down to a few key factors:

- Time
- Expertise
- Desire

2. *Expertise.* Do you have the deep knowledge and expertise needed to take those steps successfully? As you have seen, creating a comprehensive plan around your wealth—in which all the parts work in concert—requires strong knowledge of investments, insurance, business planning, accounting, trusts and estate law, and more. Do you really possess all of the requisite skills yourself? Do you really have access to such expertise through existing relationships with the professionals you're currently working with?

3. *Desire.* Even if you are very interested in finance, the idea of spending your hours writing an estate plan probably doesn't fill you with joy. Do you really want to spend your free time dealing with the issues and tasks detailed in this book, or would you rather spend that time with family and friends, pursuing interests that give your life meaning and pleasure?

Frankly, most investors—even former entrepreneurs who have plenty of time following a liquidity event—ultimately choose to implement wealth management with the help of a financial advisor who offers a true Collaborative Wealth Management Process. An advisor who acts as your personal CFO will take on the mission-critical aspects of wealth management while working closely with you and your family to ensure that any plan or solution reflects your unique needs, goals and timeframe.

MOVING FORWARD WITH CONFIDENCE

Ultimately, you have the power and the ability to put yourself on a path to post-liquidity financial success and—most important—financial meaning. Only you can decide if Collaborative Wealth Management is the right path for you. But consider this: As someone who has created significant wealth and value throughout your life, you owe it to yourself, your family and your community to make the most of your wealth so it creates tremendous benefits and supports your deepest values.

I hope that having read this book you now feel confident, as I do, that Collaborative Wealth Management is the surest way to help you achieve all that is truly most important to you and your family. I hope you are ready to explore using our process to live your best life, on your terms—today, tomorrow and for decades to come.

IS IT TIME TO GET A SECOND OPINION ABOUT YOUR FINANCES?

I wrote this book to help successful entrepreneurs learn how they can build on their impressive accomplishments and utilize their wealth to achieve even greater things going forward—for themselves, for their families, for their communities and for the causes they support.

The fact is, your financial health should be treated as seriously as your physical health. For example, say you were diagnosed with a major medical condition and given a treatment plan. Chances are you would seek out a second opinion. It's not because you don't trust your first doctor; it's because you want to be as well-informed as possible about your condition and the treatment options available. You want to be sure that you're getting all the key information you need to make a truly informed decision that is in your best interests. Different points of view can help you as you consider (or confirm) your course of action.

For those same reasons, it can be valuable to get a second opinion about your financial situation from a best-in-class wealth manager—a true professional who has the capabilities and competence to serve as your personal CFO. Research from CEG Worldwide found that just 6.6 percent of financial advisors (one out of every 16) offer clients a wealth management solution like we have outlined in the preceding chapters of this book.

At this stage of your personal and business life, it's natural to wonder if your current financial plan is going to get you where you want to be in the future. It's natural to wonder if the financial advice you are currently receiving is the best advice for your unique situation and needs. That's often the case among successful entrepreneurs like you, whose situations and needs tend to evolve and grow more complex as they become wealthier and more successful. In such instances, you may need additional help or direction.

A second opinion assessment should be designed to help you understand clearly where you are today, where you want to be down the road and whether there are any gaps in your plan that need to be addressed and corrected. Therefore, your second opinion should begin with an in-depth meeting such as the Mutual Discovery Meeting outlined in Chapter 2. This is an opportunity for an advisor to listen closely to your concerns and ask you questions about what is most important to you, in order to "diagnose" your current financial situation.

Ideally, this meeting will confirm whether or not you are on track to meet your values and goals. If so, a best-in-class wealth manager will tell you as much—and will recommend that you continue to move forward with your current plan and your current advisors.

If you are **not** ideally positioned to meet your goals, or if you are getting subpar advice, then the wealth manager should suggest ways for you to get on the right path. For example, the wealth manager may recommend that you work with his or her firm—but only if the wealth manager believes his or her firm can bring substantial value to your financial life. Conversely, he or she may recommend another advisor who is more suitable for your specific needs and situation, and introduce you.

A second opinion assessment should be designed to help you understand clearly where you are today, where you want to be down the road and whether there are any gaps in your plan that need to be addressed and corrected.

Keep in mind that very few financial advisors practicing today offer this type of detailed analysis and approach. Again, just 6 percent of advisors have adopted the Collaborative Wealth Management process as defined in this book.

If you wish to engage a second opinion about your financial situation, I have several wealth managers in my network across the U.S., and can get you pointed in the right direction. If you would like to learn more, please visit my website at liquidityandyou.com.

Appendix

PHILANTHROPY AND THE TECH ENTREPRENEUR: 3 SMART WAYS TO USE YOUR WEALTH FOR MAXIMUM SOCIAL IMPACT

Key Takeaways:

■ Tech entrepreneurs are embracing philanthropy to solve key global challenges.

■ Private foundations and donor-advised funds are two smart, tax-efficient philanthropic tools for entrepreneurs wanting their wealth to have a lifelong social impact.

■ The "Zuckerberg model" of funding both charities and for-profit companies via an LLC is a relatively new twist on traditional giving methods.

■ Selecting the right approach to charitable giving requires careful consideration of the pros and cons of the various giving vehicles.

Philanthropy in the tech world made big headlines late last year when Facebook CEO Mark Zuckerberg announced his intention to give away 99 percent of his company stock during his lifetime to fund charities, private companies and other organizations aimed at creating social good.

Zuckerberg's massive pledge (his shares were worth a whopping $45 billion at the time of the announcement) is the biggest yet in a growing movement among young tech entrepreneurs to use their wealth as a force for positive social impact. These industry leaders, many of them Millennials and Gen Xers, are looking to join the ranks of elder tech philanthropists like Bill Gates, Gordon Moore and Jeff Bezos in an effort to solve society's key challenges.

While the Facebook CEO's declaration was timed to coincide with the season of giving, tech entrepreneurs can pursue philanthropy at any time of year. Professionally, one of the greatest joys which I am most passionate about is when one of our tech entrepreneurial clients chooses to make a dent in the charitable universe, and we have the opportunity to help them determine which of the many charitable giving options is right for them.

USING WEALTH FOR GOOD

When asked if capitalism is bad, the Dalai Lama responded simply and eloquently (I'm paraphrasing):

The ability or talent to make money is a gift, and it's what you do with that gift that determines good or bad. One of the best illustrations of this is the well-known philanthropist John D. Rockefeller, whose catalyst for his giving is fascinating. In his 50s Rockefeller showed up at his doctor looking like a withered man near the end of his life. He stressed and obsessed over the smallest of costs. An extra charge of $50 (in today's dollars) caused by something uncontrollable—like a delay in shipping due to weather—would lead to a restless night. The physician gave Rockefeller an order: Stop working or you will die. By that point Rockefeller had amassed a fortune to last many lifetimes, and he decided to start giving back. However, because of his not-so-nice (some would say tyrannical) reputation, his initial attempts at philanthropy were met with cold shoulders. He kept at it and, slowly over time, the community started to accept his generosity. Rockefeller lived out the remainder of his life giving away more than $530 million. Ultimately, that philanthropic focus restored Rockefeller's health: He lived to age 97. Charitable giving options for affluent tech entrepreneurs

Whether or not you are willing and able to give in a Rockefeller-esque manner, you need to select the right charitable vehicle. That requires a working knowledge of the key characteristics—the pros and cons— of various philanthropic tools at your disposal. Most philanthropically-inclined tech entrepreneurs want to start making a difference as soon as possible. With that in mind, there are two main giving tools that are best suited to entrepreneurs looking to have a meaningful social and charitable impact during their lifetimes: Private foundations and donor advised funds.

1. Private foundations. Private foundations are independent organizations that offer philanthropists the most control and flexibility of any charitable vehicle over how the money earmarked for charity gets invested and donated.

Example: In general, donors who set up an IRS-approved private foundation can allocate money to the investments of their choice so the pool of assets can grow over time, and can choose any registered charity to receive donations—a level of freedom that's unique among charitable vehicles.

What's more, private foundations offer tax breaks that may be attractive to entrepreneurs—especially those looking to mitigate their tax burden in the wake of a liquidity event. Cash donations to private foundation are deductible up to 30 percent of the donor's adjusted gross income, while gifts of stock or real property are deductible up to 20 percent.

Private foundations also can exist in perpetuity—they have no expiration date—thus making them ideal for entrepreneurs looking to create a family charitable legacy by involving children and other heirs in the giving process over many decades.

That said, the flexibility of a private foundation comes with costs and complexities. Private foundations are expensive to maintain because they require a board of directors, IRS filings and other extensive ongoing reporting and documentation duties. An initial contribution of at least $2 million is typically needed for a private foundation to make financial sense.

Perhaps most important is the rule that private foundations must pay out at least 5 percent of their assets in grants and administrative fees annually. In other words, the assets can't remain idle. That means donors need to have a strong philanthropic vision and mission in place before they start, and be actively involved in the giving process for a private foundation to work.

Given these complexities, it's not surprising that setting up and running a private foundation so it's both effective and compliant with the regulations takes the right team— which might include consultants on grantmaking and back office personnel to handle paperwork.

2. Donor Advised Funds. At the other end of the charitable giving spectrum is the donor advised fund (DAF).

A much simpler and streamlined approach to

philanthropy, a DAF is essentially a charitable investment account available through a number of "sponsoring organizations"—including community foundations, public charities and the philanthropic arms of major investment firms such as Fidelity, Schwab and Vanguard. A DAF also takes less capital to get started than a private foundation: The required minimum initial contribution may be as low as $5,000.

Donors can set up and fund a DAF in no time. Because it's run through a sponsoring organization, a DAF doesn't require donors to deal with much paperwork—nor any of the administration and reporting duties inherent in a private foundation. That makes DAFs a potentially good option for donors who want to take a relatively hands-off approach to philanthropy.

What's more, DAFs' tax benefits are even better than those of private foundations. Generally, cash donations to a DAF can be deducted up to 50 percent of the donor's AGI (and 30% for gifts of stock and real property).

Perhaps most intriguing: Unlike private foundations, DAFs have no rules about the timing or the amount of donations. Donors can take years if they want to decide which charities to support. This feature makes the DAF especially appealing to donors and families that want to fund a charitable vehicle right away to get an immediately tax benefit, but who haven't figured out where they want that money to go.

The cons? DAF donors have far less control over the money they donate than they would with a foundation. Technically, they can only advise the firm sponsoring the DAF to send money to the charity or charities they wish to support. In practice, most requests are accepted—but the bottom line is that the sponsoring organization has final say.

Donors also have less control over how the money in their DAFs is invested. The options might include just a limited number of mutual funds and ETFs, for example, and the sponsoring organization makes the big picture investment decisions about asset allocation, rebalancing and the like.

In addition, DAFs don't enable families to build long-term charitable legacies involving multiple generations. That's because the sponsoring organizations tend to restrict or limit the ability of donors' heirs to make recommendations about how the funds' assets should be donated.

At the end of the day, the decision about which vehicle to use rests largely on how involved a donor wants to be in the giving process as well as the latitude and ability to gift. Oftentimes families will opt to fund both types of vehicles—or start with a DAF to "dip their toes in the water" and later set up a more involved private foundation after they have more experience and a clearer philanthropic vision for their wealth.

AN ALTERNATIVE APPROACH TO PHILANTHROPY WITH TREMENDOUS BENEFITS

There also are options that aren't entirely philanthropy-based, but which still are designed to support causes and interests about which people are passionate. For example, you can do what Zuckerberg (and Ebay's Pierre Omidyar before him) did: Set up a Limited Liability Company (LLC). This approach comes with no tax deductions—none at all—because it's technically a corporate structure and not a charitable tool. So why do it? Tremendous freedom and social impact. A sort-of "private foundation 2.0," the LLC structure allows philanthropists to use their money just about any way they see fit—including as investments in for-profit companies that are trying to solve societal challenges. In contrast, foundations and DAFs only allow donors to make grants to tax-exempt nonprofits. Likewise, an LLC is allowed to spend its assets on lobbying and political donations—actions that strictly charitable vehicles can't take. As Zuck himself posted on Facebook: "By using an LLC instead of a traditional foundation, we receive no tax benefit from transferring our shares…but we gain flexibility to execute our mission more effectively."

CONCLUSION

Clearly, choosing the right giving mechanism is not a decision that can be made quickly or rashly, given the complexities and details of the various charitable tools.

Entrepreneurs should always consult with their financial and tax advisors before deciding how philanthropic values can fit in with the larger wealth picture. The right approach can help set up entrepreneurs to maximize their social impact on the causes they care about most—while also ensuring that they remain well-positioned to achieve their full range of financial goals for themselves and their families.

ENDNOTES

Chapter 1

1. U.S. Census Bureau. (2015). *Statistics for All U.S. Firms by Industry, Gender, Ethnicity, and Race for the U.S., States, Metro Areas, Counties, and Places: 2012.* Retrieved from https://factfinder. census.gov/bkmk/table/1.0/en/SBO/2012/00CSA03//naics~624.

2. State & Federal Earned Income Tax Credits. (2015). Retrieved from http://www.csd.ca.gov/ Services/EarnedIncomeTaxCredit.aspx.

3. Surveyed by Prince Associates.

Chapter 4

4. The Vanguard Group, Inc. (2014). *Today's affluent investors: insights and opportunities.* Retrieved from https://static1.squarespace.com/static/56f9b1fc746fb96413a0fcbc/t/57c09a1f-2994caf99f0ae077/1472240185542/VanguardStudy-HealthCarePlanning.pdf.

5. Family Business Institute. (2017). *Succession Planning.* Retrieved from http://www.familybusi-nessinstitute.com/index.php/Succession-Planning/.

6. Hargreaves, S. (2014, June 25). *Squandering the family fortune: Why rich families are losing money.* Retrieved from http://money.cnn.com/2014/06/25/luxury/family-wealth.

GLOSSARY

1. **Actuary:** A professional who deals with the management and assessment of risk on insurance policies, financial investments, and any other financial ventures.

2. **Andrew Carnegie:** Identified as one of the modern world's richest people ever, Carnegie was a Scottish-American industrialist who championed the American steel industry in the late 1800s. He is known for advising to "put all your eggs in one basket, and then watch that basket."

3. **Art professional:** A specialist employed to help their clients with acquisition, disposition, protection, valuation and tax mitigation related to the sale and transfer of their art collection(s).

4. **Asset class:** A group of securities categorized by similar behavior and subject to the same laws and regulations. Examples would be equities (stocks), fixed income (bonds) and cash equivalents (money market instruments).

5. **Asset restructuring:** Restructuring is action taken to significantly modify the structure and obligations of an entity in order to improve it.

6. **Berkshire Hathaway Inc:** A holding company for a large number of businesses run by Warren Buffet.

Beginning as a small group of textile milling plants in Omaha, Nebraska, it started to shift when Buffett became the controlling shareholder in the 1960s and began to direct the proceeds from the core business into diversified investments. Warren Buffet now serves as Chairman and CEO.

7. **Bonds:** A form of investment in which an investor loans money to an entity (typically the government or a corporation) for a defined period of time.

8. **Business broker:** A professional who specializes in providing help for individuals and companies who want to buy or sell a business. Many specialize in a specific industry, such as retail, hospitality, manufacturing or restaurants.

9. **Buy-sell agreements:** A legally binding agreement between the owners of a business that sets asset transfer guidelines in case of an owner's death or exit from the business. Also known as a buyout agreement.

10. **Capital gains**
    a.) **Short-term:** Realized by the sale or exchange of a capital asset that has been held for exactly one year or less. Taxed at the top marginal tax rate, and can only be reduced by realizing a short-term loss.

b.) Long-term: Realized by the sale or exchange of a capital asset that has been held for more than one year. The taxable amount is determined by the amount gained (or lost) when the investor sells the asset. The tax rate is typically lower than that of short-term gains.

11. **Capital gains tax:** Tax imposed on the profits realized through the sale of an asset, specifically when an investor or a corporation sells an asset for more than its purchase price.

12. **Charitable lead trust:** A trust created to reduce the taxable income of the beneficiary. It works by donating a portion of its income to a chosen charity and then transferring the remainder of the trust to its beneficiaries after a designated period of time.

13. **Charitable remainder trust:** An irrevocable trust created to reduce the taxable income of both the grantor and the beneficiary. The trust is tax-exempt and works by dispersing income to the beneficiaries for a designated period of time, followed by donating the remainder of the trust to a chosen charity.

14. **Charlie Munger:** Vice Chairman of Berkshire Hathaway and Warren Buffett's right-hand man, Munger is an American investor, businessman, and philanthropist. An expert in his own right, it is said that

every investment decision that Buffett makes requires the agreement of Mr. Munger.

15. **Classic index fund:** A type of mutual fund with a portfolio constructed to match the performance of a market index, e.g. the S&P 500. Typically, index funds boast broad market exposure, low portfolio turnover, and low operating expenses. *See 'passive investing'.*

16. **Credit expert:** A professional who can monitor and comprehensively evaluate their clients' current credit situation, often relating to any loans that their clients are carrying.

17. **Credit-shelter trust:** A type of trust fund allowing married couples to reduce estate taxes by taking full advantage of state and federal estate tax exemptions. Typically only available to multimillion-dollar estate holders.

18. **Derivatives specialist:** Derivatives are financial instruments whose value is dependent on the value of another "underlying" asset. Derivatives specialists can help clients manage certain risks, such as concentrated stock positions.

19. **DFA (Dimensional Fund Advisors):** A global investment manager dedicated to maximizing investor performance through the implementation of rigorous academic research. We believe DFA to be the best institutional-quality solution for our clients.

20. **Donor-advised fund:** A private fund created to manage charitable donations on behalf of an organization, family or individual.

21. **"Drag" (on portfolio):** On an investment portfolio, referring to the negative effect of transaction costs and taxes on investment performance.

22. **Estate planning:** The preparation tasks required to manage an individual's assets in the event of their incapacitation or death. This includes allocating certain assets to their heirs and the settlement of estate taxes, among other requirements pertaining to the individual's unique situation.

23. **Estate tax:** Tax imposed on assets left to heirs in excess of limits set by law. It does not apply to the transfer of assets to a surviving spouse.

24. **Eugene Fama:** An American economist and Nobel Laureate. Referred to by some as "The Father of Finance," Fama is best known for his groundbreaking work on asset pricing, stock market behavior, and portfolio theory. He also serves as a consultant on the Board of Directors at Dimensional Fund Advisors and is a professor at the University of Chicago.

25. **Family governance professional:** Family governance refers to both the governance of a business and the related family. A family governance

professional can be vitally important in dealing with complex family wealth issues.

26. **Fiduciary:** An entity bound by ethics to act in the best interests of its beneficiary. For example, as a fiduciary, a financial advisory firm is required by law to act in its clients' best interests—never its own. This means it cannot be influenced by commissions, kick-backs or other incentives for steering its clients into any specific fund.

27. **Financial therapist:** Through both psychology and fiscal expertise, financial therapists work exclusively with the human side of one's financial life. We've found that the right professional can help clients deal with the changes that come with liquidity events.

28. **Four key drivers of investment success:** Return, Risk, Costs, Taxes.

29. **Fund turnover:** Usually reported for a 12-month time period, fund turnover is calculated by dividing the total amount of securities purchased or sold (whichever is less) by the total value (NAV, or Net Asset Value) of the fund.

30. **Generation-skipping trust:** A legally binding agree-ment in which the assets included are passed down to the owner (or grantor)'s grandchildren, as opposed to their children. It can be used as a tool to avoid cer-tain estate tax obligations.

31. **Gift tax:** Tax imposed on the individual giving anything of a legally specified value to another person. The gift giver is required to pay the gift tax.

32. **Government-sponsored enterprise:** GSEs are privately run corporations with public purposes. They were originally created by the U.S. Congress to reduce the cost for certain borrowing sectors within the United States economy, specifically for students, farmers and homeowners.

   a.) **Fannie Mae:** Short for the Federal National Mortgage Association (FNMA). The FNMA is a GSE founded by Congress during the Great Depression to stimulate the housing market by making more mortgages available to moderate-to-low-income borrowers.

   b.) **Freddie Mac:** Short for the Federal Home Loan Mortgage Corporation (FHLMC). The FHLMC is a GSE created in 1970 to expand the secondary market for mortgages in the US.

33. **Health and wellness professional:** Often in the form of a Wellness Concierge, a health and wellness professional refers to an expert in the world of healthcare who can be consulted and employed to ensure that clients and their families are getting full access to the premiere medical services available today.

34. **High-risk investment:** An investment in which there is a high chance of loss.

35. **Household balance sheet:** A balance sheet is a financial statement summarizing a company's assets, liabilities, and shareholder's equity at a given point in time. It provides insight to investors on what the company owns, owes, and is worth. A household balance sheet is similar, designed to give its owner an idea of their own personal assets, liabilities and net worth. This may include a personal investment portfolio, real estate, and other assets and/or business interests.

36. **Income tax:** Tax imposed on the annual financial earnings of individuals, corporations, trusts and other legal entities.

37. **Interest rate:** The proportion of a loan that is charged as interest to the borrower, usually expressed as an annual percentage of the balance of the loan.

38. **IPO:** Initial public offering. "Going public" occurs when a private company first becomes listed for trading on a public exchange.

39. **IRD (income in respect of a decedent):** Money that was due to a decedent—or deceased—that is applied to the recipient or estate as taxable income.

40. **John Bogle:** The founder and retired chief executive of Vanguard, Bogle is an American investor, business

magnate, and philanthropist. He serves the general investing public as an advocate for accessible investing by providing a vehicle for low-cost diversification.

41. **Ken French:** Co-author of well-known economic research with Eugene Fama, French is an expert on the behavior of security prices and investment strategies. He also serves as a consultant on the Board of Directors at Dimensional Fund Advisors and is a Distinguished Professor of Finance at the Tuck School of Business at Dartmouth College.

42. **Liquidity event:** The merger, purchase or sale of a corporation or an IPO (initial public offering). Typically, this converts the equity held by a company's founders and investors into cash, making it a common exit strategy. More broadly, a liquidity event can also describe less common transfers of ownership that may not include cash proceeds.

43. **LLC (Limited Liability Company):** A corporate structure designed to protect its members from being held personally liable for any company debts or liabilities.

44. **M&A attorneys:** Legal professionals who specialize in mergers and acquisitions, or the consolidation of companies and assets.

45. **Mark Cuban:** Owner of the NBA's Dallas Mavericks and co-owner of 2929 Entertainment, Cuban is an

American investor, businessman, author, television personality, and philanthropist. He speaks frequently on his propensity to act on his "competitive engine."

46. **P&C insurance:** Property and casualty insurance protects what the policyholder owns (property, or assets) while protecting them financially in the event of a lawsuit. Common forms of P&C insurance include homeowner's insurance, renter's insurance, auto insurance, and umbrella insurance policies.

47. **Passive investing:** An investment strategy that keeps buying and selling to a minimum in order to maximize long-term returns. Passive investing aims to build slow, steady wealth over time by attempting to track the performance of a market-weighted index.

48. **Personal lines insurance specialist:** Personal lines insurance refers to property and casualty insurance products for individuals. A personal lines insurance specialist is an expert in the world of P&C insurance, typically working at the very high end of the market.

49. **Portfolio expense ratio:** The annual fee that all mutual funds or ETFs charge their shareholders. It is calculated by dividing the operating expenses of the mutual fund by the average dollar value of all assets within the fund.

50. **Private equity firm**: Private equity is capital that is composed of funds and investors that directly invest

in private companies, and is not noted on a public exchange. A private equity firm is an investment management company that invests in private equity through a variety of investment strategies.

51. **Private foundation:** A nonprofit organization, typically created by a single primary donation from an individual or entity. Its funds and programs are managed by its own designated trustees and/or directors.

52. **Probate service:** Probate refers to the legal process implemented to determine whether a will is authentic and valid, as well as to the general administering of a deceased person's estate. Probate services help to assist responsible parties with getting through the probate process.

53. **QSSB rule:** A portion of the United States tax code that allows for partial exclusion for gain from certain small business stock, potentially alleviating the tax payer of 100% of their tax burden.

54. **Remainder purchase marital trust:** An estate planning tool that allows its owner to provide for their spouse and their children at the same time. Its purpose is to protect its assets from the claims of a subsequent spouse. It also serves to protect its beneficiaries from estate taxes.

55. **S&P 500:** The Standard & Poor's 500 is an American stock market index that is seen as an indicator of

overall performance of U.S. equities. It is comprised of 500 of the largest companies listed on the NYSE and NASDAQ.

56. **Securities lawyer:** A security is an asset that holds monetary value and typically represents an ownership or creditor relationship. A securities lawyer frequently represents clients in the transactional work involved with various public and private securities transactions.

57. **Self-cancelling installment note:** A promissory note—a legal document containing a written promise to pay a specified sum to a specified payee on a certain date — that is canceled upon the death of the payee.

58. **"Silo" advisor:** A silo refers to an information system that is unable to freely work with others due to isolation. A silo advisor fails to coordinate their efforts with other professionals working on their clients' teams. While this may make it easier for them to implement their own quick solutions without having to consider others' insight, it also means that the choices they make may not be fully informed.

59. **Single-company risk:** The financial uncertainty undertaken by an investor who holds a disproportionate ownership interest in one specific firm. The solution is diversification: by investing in additional—and uncorrelated—companies and assets, investors can

mitigate the potentially negative impact of a single company or asset's performance.

60. **Stocks:** A form of security that indicates ownership in a corporation, and entitles its owner to a claim on a portion of the corporation's assets and earnings.

61. **Ted Turner:** An American media mogul and a philanthropist known for founding CNN, the world's first 24-hour cable news channel. As an investor, Turner made headlines when he lost $8 billion that he had concentrated in the stock of AOL Time Warner.

62. **"Think Tank":** A formal panel of experts that meets regularly to brainstorm and implement strategic—and often complex—solutions for clients. Also referred to as an advisor's "expert team."

63. **Trading costs:** Transaction costs in the form of commissions and fees charged by portfolio managers for their role in managing clients' investments.

64. **Traditional life insurance:** Also called whole life, a policy that pays out to its contracted beneficiaries upon the death of the contract holder. This differs from term life insurance, which only covers the contract holder until an age limit specified within the contract.

65. **Trust:** A legal relationship in which one party (the trustor) gives another party (the trustee) the right to

govern over specified property or assets for the benefit of a third party (the beneficiary).

66. **Trustees (successor managers):** A person or firm charged with administering and distributing assets on behalf of a third party. While common in estate planning, trustees can also be delegated in the event of bankruptcy, for a charity, for a trust fund, or for certain retirement plans or pensions.

67. **Umbrella policy:** Extra liability coverage that goes beyond what is covered by P&C insurance, designed to protect the policyholder from lawsuits, vandalism, libel, slander and invasion of privacy. The added coverage is most useful for individuals who own exceptionally expensive assets and are at higher risk of being sued.

68. **Valuation specialist:** A professional who specializes in calculating the fair market value of publicly-traded securities and privately-held assets.

69. **Vanguard:** An investment management company with over $4 trillion in AUM. The largest provider of mutual funds and the second-largest provider of exchange-traded funds worldwide, we consider Vanguard to be one of the best retail solutions on the market for the average investor.

70. **Warren Buffett:** One of the most successful investors in the world, Buffett is an American business magnate, investor, and philanthropist. At press, Buffet is the second wealthiest person in the United States, and the fourth wealthiest in the world. He advocates for wealth preservation, reminding us that the #1 rule of investing is simply not to lose money.

71. **Will:** A legally enforceable declaration of how one wants their property or assets to be distributed in the event of their death. Also known as a Last Will and Testament.

72. **"Wrapper":** Insurance wrappers are instruments into which investors can place stocks, hedge funds or virtually any other assets, allowing them to lessen the tax on investment income.

ACKNOWLEDGMENTS

A special thank you to Brian and Rommia for their patience and persistence to make this book a reality.

Dr. Andy, BDS, Bobbie, and everyone that believed in me early on.

TSK for his support when my journey started.

Glenn, Paul, Pat Pat, and others for getting me to stop "thinking" and start doing.

W. Clement Stone, whose message permanently altered my life.

To you, the readers, who use your money to make the world a better place.